To finder of This
Book — please Read
and pass along

THE ART OF
SPIRITUAL
WARFARE

THE ART OF SPIRITUAL WARFARE

A Guide to Lasting Inner Peace
Based on Sun Tzu's
The Art of War

GRANT SCHNARR

A publication supported by
THE KERN FOUNDATION

Quest Books
Theosophical Publishing House
Wheaton, Illinois ♦ Chennai (Madras), India

The Theosophical Publishing House
P. O. Box 270
Wheaton, IL 60189-0270

A publication of the Theosophical Publishing House,
a department of the Theosophical Society in America

Library of Congress Cataloging-in-Publication Data

Schnarr, Grant R.
    The art of spiritual warfare: a guide to lasting inner
peace based on Sun Tzu's The art of war / Grant Schnarr.
— 1st Quest ed.
        p.   cm.
Includes bibliographical references.
ISBN 0-8356-0787-9
1. Spiritual life.   2. Spiritual warfare. 3. Sun-tzu,
6th cent. B.C. The art of war.   I. Title.
BL624.S35 2000
291.4'4—dc21   00-037781

5   4   3   2   *   01   02   03   04   05   06   07

Printed in the United States of America

For my four sons,

who are growing into true spiritual warriors:

Ronald, Jason, Owen, Steven

Contents

Acknowledgments

This book could not have been written without the foundational wisdom of Sun Tzu, whose 2500-year-old sayings are as relevant today as ever, especially when read on a spiritual level. The excerpts from Sun Tzu's *The Art of War,* which precede each chapter, are taken from a translation by the Reverend Jon Jin, whose careful and tedious work is much appreciated. I have also relied on two other translations for comparison: Thomas Cleary's translation, Shambhala Publications, Boston, 1991; and Roger Ames's translation, Ballantine Books, New York, 1993. I thank Robert Moore for his inspiration and encouragement in writing this book. His work has been life changing to so many. I am indebted to him for his help. I also thank Ray Silverman for his original editing and enthusiasm about the text.

Foreword

*I*t takes an extremely bold person to suggest in these times that we should be utilizing the imagery of spiritual warfare and spiritual combat to discuss an appropriate, even *centrally important* aspect, of the praxis of human spirituality. By publishing this book, Grant Schnarr is demonstrating a refreshing boldness. For an author to begin to address this topic in our contemporary context he must be willing to engage and challenge some of the most established and cherished—yet dangerously misguided—assumptions of contemporary ideology, theology, psychology, and spirituality. Each of these areas of discourse in recent years has been quick to try to solve the problems of human violence by eliminating the word "warrior" from our approved lexicon. According to this popular agenda, the elimination of human violence and destructive behaviors will be achieved by purging religious discourse—even hymnody—of any reference to war or combat . . . and implying that anyone who speaks of spiritual warfare or uses martial imagery or suggests that we think of spiritual "strategy" or "tactics" is thereby causing violence and colluding with the worst in human nature and/or culture. It would be hard to overemphasize the extent of the simplistic and naive acceptance of such a point of view.

What is lost when we have a theory of change which assumes that not speaking of an aspect of the human psyche and behavior will make it go away? What happens when our approach to spirituality does not include the capacity to image the spiritual life in terms of desperate combat? Let me share a few reflections.

First, only those who have not benefited from the revolution in consciousness brought about by the various traditions of depth psychology will continue to adhere to a theory of change as naive as the Enlightenment mind and its contemporary derivatives. Once one is aware of the dynamics of repression and denial (and the other ego defense mechanisms) one will not be so sure that aggression which is out of sight (not verbalized as such) will be out of mind (not present and active in the unconscious and in behavior). *In short, we can never hope to deal with the enormity of the problem of human aggression by "cleaning up" our language and assuming that the mythic images relating to human instincts have now disappeared and are no longer functional.* This is where Carl Jung's emphasis on facing the objective reality of the psyche and its collective archetypal contents is so important. Following Jung's tradition I have spent a great deal of time in my psychoanalytic research and writing showing the way in which the collective unconscious contains the archetypal imagery of the warrior and that aggression is, in fact, one of the four major building blocks of a healthy and mature human self—male or female.

From the point of view of a Jungian structural psychoanalysis, the question is not one of a naive fantasy of eliminating human aggression by not thinking it, but rather of facing the reality of the role of aggression in the psyche and of finding appropriate channels for its mature expression in service and leadership toward a just and humane future. Just as the king/queen archetype, not counterbalanced by a prophetic and wise magician archetype, leads to tyranny and the arrogance of power, the lover archetype, not balanced by a fully empowered and integrated warrior archetype, can lead to naivete, masochism, and unwitting collusion with the agendas of evil agencies both within the psyche and in the social world.

The question of the reality of Radical Evil is an especially important one when considering questions of spiritual warfare. Carl Jung courageously challenged the theologians of his day who tended to reduce evil to a theological concept, avoiding facing its terrible agency in our lives. He called upon us to recognize the enormous power of Radical Evil, both within us and in the outer world. He saw our personal and spiritual development as a struggle for consciousness of evil and emphasized the importance of developing the courage to face it. In fact, the most basic fundamentals of spiritual discernment are dependent upon an adequate accessing of the potentials of the warrior archetype in the human psyche. Without drawing upon the warrior archetype in the human psyche, rather than doing away with evil one *is merely in massive denial as to its existence.* When asked to define what it means to be a warrior, I have often answered, "Warriors fight evil, often at the risk of their own well-being." If one cannot discern the presence of evil, one certainly cannot oppose it . . . and without the development of the warrior within, one will almost certainly be ineffectual in the struggle against it.

Grant Schnarr has written a profound introductory "training manual" for the person new to spiritual combat. He has updated traditional insights to help us in our struggle to live with integrity, courage, and faithfulness to our spiritual values and commitments—our most fundamental mission. I am indebted to him for his contribution and honored to give it my enthusiastic endorsement.

—Robert L. Moore, Ph.D.

Introduction

You and I are called to a battle as old as humankind and yet as relevant as the breath you are about to take. It is, perhaps, the only noble battle, because it is not about killing, taking land, playing the part of an aggressor, or gaining the upper hand over people. It isn't even about learning how to be tougher and defending personal boundaries and emotional space. Rather, the battle that calls us is the fight for inner personal freedom, spiritual health, love, goodness, and growth. It is the battle for the well-being of our own spirits and for the recovery of our souls. It is the struggle for spirituality, a struggle which can bring lasting peace to ourselves and to the world.

Everyone struggles with personal demons, destructive tendencies which not only create unhappiness, but produce incredible pain. But victory over such spiritual enemies is also possible, and with it, spiritual peace. In my own life, the struggle to overcome addictive behavior and the character defects associated with an addictive personality has been a tough battle. It seems that no sooner than I have vanquished one enemy to my spiritual well-being, another rushes over the hill in a full-out attack. Sometimes I've been able to see spiritual enemies coming and prepare for their assault on my soul. At other times, I've been taken completely by surprise and had to scramble to muster my own personal forces against them. I haven't always won. There have been some humiliating defeats, but with the help of the Divine and a humble heart which is ready to get up and go at it again, I've won more victories than I've lost. As a result, I'm claiming new ground every day, and with it, a new freedom and inner peace.

Where I've found help with fighting my own personal demons has been in the great religions and spiritual philosophies of the world—everything from the Bible to the *Tao Te*

1

Ching, from the Koran to the Bhagavad-Gita, from the spiritual teachings of Emanuel Swedenborg to Native American folk legends. What is amazing is how so many different religions and spiritual disciplines say the same things. They acknowledge the spiritual struggles within and share incredible wisdom about waging war against our inward spiritual enemies. For many, these personal demons have their origin in a spiritual realm. They are not just human shortcomings, but subtle enemies operating through our shortcomings; they are not simply bouts of ignorance, but assaults from forces of darkness. In many of these ancient religions and spiritual philosophies, such as, for example, Zoroastrianism or Manichaeanism, it is described as the war between good and evil.

I personally don't believe that one primary devil is orchestrating spiritual armies against the heavenly host. But I do believe in the war between good and evil. I have no choice. I've experienced it in my own being ever since I was a youth. I've not only witnessed but *felt* the angels and devils struggling for charge over my soul. I've been intimately involved in every battle, through my choices, longings, struggles, and dark nights of the soul. I've witnessed this battle play itself out in a world which seems on the brink of open spiritual warfare, a world in which brutality, injustice, and inhumanity wage war against compassion, mercy, and love. I personally believe that these are spiritual forces struggling with one another, struggling to gain ground in each human heart and in the world at large. I know that if I do my part by fighting the battles against the darker forces within my own being, I not only help myself, but through my meager efforts, allow more light to shine and more love to flow in the world.

Think about what a difference it would make if each individual made a commitment to oppose what is destructive in his or her life and pledged to work for the betterment of self and the world. It would have an incredible impact on each individual and on society as a whole. Isn't that the real and noble cause of every major religion and spiritual philosophy? This is the cause which makes us all one people, in one faith, pledged to one God, whom we call different names.

Whether we know for a fact that these battling forces emanate from spiritual realms or personify conflicting animal instincts doesn't make much difference to our spiritual growth and happiness. But to regard destructive tendencies as personal enemies helps distance us from them. It gives us a clearer picture of what these tendencies are and how they work destruction in our lives, while at the same time empowering us to rid ourselves of them. Therefore, it is enough for us to acknowledge the forces of darkness and to fight against them to make ourselves better people and the world a better place. Once we do that, the mission becomes clear, the enemy becomes clear, and the task is at hand. The trumpet has sounded, and we are called to spiritual battle.

More and more people are recognizing the reality of spiritual warfare, and many books have recently been written about the spiritual warrior. Some are very good at describing the warrior's disposition, attitudes, and actions, and some touch upon the battle of defending one's boundaries or fighting for one's cause. However, most don't talk about the spiritual battle itself. Perhaps this is because people are afraid that their message will be misconstrued as a return to dogmatic religion or spiritual fables which no longer work in modern society. Perhaps people just don't know much about the battle, so they don't talk about it. This is unfortunate, because the battle is what the spiritual warrior is all about. It is through the battle that the spiritual warrior grows and effects change in the self and in the world. Through spiritual battle the warrior is borne, shaped, and molded into the noble soldier. Through victory, the warrior is transformed, and so also is a fraction of the world, into something better.

This book, *The Art of Spiritual Warfare*, is about the inward battle itself. It is about the struggle and the strategy, the insight and the inspiration, and how, when, and where to fight. It calls upon the wisdom of the greatest spiritual warriors of the ages, those who have struggled to defeat the darker forces within and sought to make their world a better place.

I have structured this wisdom around that of perhaps the best book on warfare ever written: Sun Tzu's *The Art of War*. This two-thousand-year-old book has long been recognized as one of the most important treatises ever written on the strategy of warfare. Its principles have been studied and adopted by military generals throughout history, from ancient battles in China, to the wars of Napoleon, to modern world wars. I came across Sun Tzu's work by accident. I first saw it on a friend's book shelf in Colorado. The title jumped out at me. I remember leafing through the book in my friend's home, eagerly glancing at the index, studying the chapter headings. Something about it drew me. I realized that what I held in my hand was not just a book about military strategy, but a parable for dealing with my own life. I had long battled my own demons through twelve-step programs and other support networks, and I was familiar with the real struggle to live a life of love and integrity. In this age-old book of battle strategies for the outer *physical* plane, I immediately recognized the potential for help on the spiritual plane. The same principles hold true, whether the war is without or within.

Here are some of the lessons of Sun Tzu which jumped out at me:

> If you know the enemy and yourself you will not be at
> risk in a hundred battles.
> Stay on ground which is unassailable to the enemy.
> To fight any battle without a strategy is to throw away
> the victory.
> The one who goes into battle aware will claim the victory.
> Timing is important in confronting enemies.
> Know when to fight and not to fight.
> Know the terrain in which you do battle.
> Calm and decisiveness are critical in the heat of battle.
> A good general walks in the Way (Tao).

Each of these and many other lessons have taught me something about confronting my own personal demons and mastering myself. For instance, one of my greatest spiritual enemies is an overwhelming need to control my world. Yes, I tend to be a control freak. Much of this characteristic comes from having grown up with an alcoholic father whose mood and actions were often unpredictable. I had it fairly well drilled into me by experience that I had better control my world if I want to protect myself. The desire for total control can drive me crazy by filling me with fears that what I don't control will hurt or even attack me. This spiritual enemy would have me believe that others cannot be trusted, that I have to do it, whatever it may be, all by myself. This becomes a trap, because there is always too much to do and too many variables that I cannot control.

Paying attention to this enemy, learning its every move, its strengths and weaknesses, helps me to defeat it. I don't simply react from fear now when circumstances arise that are out of my control. When I feel that desire loom up within me, I am able to see it coming. The warning trumpet sounds. I say, "There it is, the fear. I don't have to be fearful." Part of my spiritual work is in getting to know and recognize this enemy. I also learn to recognize the situations in which I am most vulnerable. I know, for instance, that in any kind of planning for the future with someone, where I have a stake in the outcome, I will tend to fall into a battle for control. Knowing this terrain, I can prepare myself before entering it. I can try to stay on ground which is unassailable to this enemy of fear and control.

In applying these and other such principles, I found that the battles I faced became less prolonged and ended more often in victory than in stalemate or defeat. I found as well that I was able to avoid many needless struggles and enjoy a great deal more peace in my life. My spiritual growth truly accelerated on all levels. In sharing this approach through classes, seminars, and retreats, I have found it to be a great benefit to others. My hope in putting this book together is that it may help many more individuals in their spiritual struggles and thus be of service to the world as a whole.

I have begun each chapter of *The Art of Spiritual Warfare* with a selection from Sun Tzu's writings in order to convey the flavor of the original and also to encourage the reader to draw further insights than my own. In some places, I have used portions of the original text in the chapters themselves, because their truth, when read on a spiritual level, is priceless. I have also added tasks to the end of each chapter to help ground the spiritual insights in the real world and daily life. In thus combining principles with practical applications, I have sought to create a guidebook for spiritual warfare.

I have long sought a field guide for my own spiritual battles. In studying the ancient texts and combining their wit and wisdom, I have found one. It has helped me incredibly. In fact, I have been amazed at the new sense of freedom and power it has given me. It has allowed me to distance myself from my inner enemies, see them for what they truly are, and recognize their destructive power in my life. It has given me the courage to move with boldness and discernment against them. I now have tools at my disposal and weapons with which to defend myself against my spiritual aggressors. The guidebook has given me the strength to vanquish some enemies I never imagined defeating and the satisfaction of knowing that I can, in all reality, win the battle. My hope is that it will do the same for you. In fact, I know that if you take upon yourself the cause of personal transformation, you will find *The Art of Spiritual Warfare* to be a faithful guide, teacher, and ally in spiritual combat. You will gradually become a powerful combatant against your spiritual foes, and you will win many incredible battles in your spiritual life.

Moreover, I personally believe that the time is now. There is too much darkness in the world; too much hatred, selfishness, animality; too much pain and sorrow. I sense that the dark forces are making their last stand. But this isn't some supernatural battle on a far distant plane. It is through humanity that this destruction is wrought, and it is through humanity that it can be defeated. It begins inside you and me, and that's where it ends, too. But if the dark forces are making their move, we may be assured that heaven is also. Whether angels are real beings, or symbols of spiritual powers above and within the human soul, they are moving us to action. They are touching each one of us, arousing us from our spiritual sleep, and calling us to the battle. Michael and his angels are battling the dragon, but they need our help, because the battle takes place inside of us. It's time to hear the call, wake up, put on our armor, and fight. It's time to storm the dragon's lair within our own hearts and minds and to free ourselves from his rage. It's time to gather together to restore love to a loveless world; to let real spiritual and natural peace rest within all lands; and to allow kindness, justice, mercy, and the Divine to reign once again in our minds, hearts, and lives.

Sun Tzu said:

Military action is important to the nation—it is the ground of death and life, the path of survival and destruction, so it is imperative to examine it. Therefore, measure in terms of five things, use these assessments to make comparisons, and thus find out what the conditions are. The five things are the Way, the weather, the terrain, the leadership, and discipline. . . .

CHAPTER 1

Spiritual Assessments

Spiritual warfare is a vital matter of the human condition. It is the field upon which spiritual life and death is determined and the road that leads either to inward survival or to ruin. The outcome of this warfare determines whether one lives in unhappiness and discontent, or whether through mastering the self in spiritual struggle, one finds lasting inner peace. Intimate knowledge of the ways of spiritual combat, and the ability to fight in it, is of the utmost importance. Nothing is of more value, for the quality of one's spiritual life depends upon it.

To understand the nature of your spiritual condition and measure the outcome of any inner struggle, appraise your situation on the basis of the following five criteria advocated by Sun Tzu. The first is the Way *(Tao)*; the second is the spiritual climate; the third is the earthly terrain; the fourth is character; and the fifth is discipline.

1. The Way, or the Tao, is the organizing principle of Taoism, a religion articulated in the *Tao Te Ching* by Lao Tzu in the sixth century BC. But know that "the Tao that can be spoken is not the true Tao." The Way is infinite and unknowable in itself, and yet it must be explored by anyone seeking spiritual growth. In the nontheistic Eastern tradition, the Way is the order of life, the flow of all things, the ineffable ground of all being. In terms of Western theology, the Way is God's creation, providence, operation, grace, and peace, all wrapped up together into a resplendent One. For the spiritual warrior, it becomes a path upon which one encounters both challenges and good fortune, sorrow and joy, victory and defeat. Through acceptance and a willingness to learn and grow, the master warrior is led by the Divine. The spiritual warrior allows life to unfold and does not fight against life, but rather learns the art of surrender to the Divine, and like a child, allows the Divine to lead toward all things blessed.

The way of the spiritual warrior is a paradox. It is a struggle and it is not a struggle. It is a war against self, and yet it is not against self. It is a battle that can only be fought alone, and yet the spiritual warrior never fights alone. It is a war which the spiritual warrior cannot win, because the opposing spiritual forces are too mighty, yet victory is achieved. The master of spiritual warfare controls life and individual destiny by allowing it to unfold and reacting according to its unfolding. The expert in spiritual warfare conquers himself by discovering the darker forces which move within, not through associating with them, but opposing them. In deep spiritual struggle, the powerful warrior surrenders to higher powers to achieve victory. Fighting alone, the spiritual warrior solicits aid from allies of a higher realm who gain the victory. The master warrior acts without expectation, fights without aggression, wins without winning. This may seem like a paradox, and so it is. But study it, meditate upon it, live by it, and you will understand its truth. And for now, know this: surrender to the Divine is the first step on the Way.

2. *Spiritual climate* refers to light and darkness and their changing positions in the spiritual realm. The greatest battle is waged on this higher ground and with forces far beyond human scope and imagination. It is an eternal conflict between the powers of light and darkness, love and hatred, good and evil, and between spiritual life and death itself. It is vast and immense, and though it manifests itself in earthly conflict and strife, it plays out its greatest contests on the battlefield within

the human soul. The master warrior knows these forces and contributes to the greater victory through perseverance in the individual conflicts and inner strife. Through recognizing the forces of darkness and light, the master warrior enters this greater arena as a freedom fighter. As if awakening from deep sleep, the spiritual warrior rises to a new awareness and a new challenge: in fighting for one's own freedom, the spiritual warrior fights for all of humankind. And so it has been written of old:

> For we do not struggle against the flesh and blood,
> But against principalities,
> Against the powers,
> Against the rulers of darkness of this age,
> Against spiritual forces of evil in the heavenly realm.
>   (Ephesians 6:12)

Awareness of the higher realities in one's life and of the spiritual climate within which one resides comes easier to some than others. I have heard many say that in the darkest times they sense their destructive impulses springing from powers greater than their own which feed such impulses and direct them like troops on the battlefield of the mind and soul. I have felt this way time and again in the struggle to release myself from whatever personal demon may be attacking me. I have experienced bursts of rage, or fallen in lust, or being filled with a terror, acted irrationally. Who hasn't? But have you ever asked yourself, "How could I do that?" or said, "That just wasn't me"? This isn't just an excuse to blame someone else for our actions. It's not simply using the old line, "The devil made me do it," in order to get off the hook of responsibility. We are, indeed, responsible for our actions. But there is a driving force behind the fear and anxiety, behind the compulsiveness and desire, behind the selfishness and want. For me, these are the forces of hell working to dismantle my life and keep me a prisoner, while God and angels fight for my soul. Knowing this helps me not to identify with the destructive tendencies within me. I can side with the Divine and the forces of good, fight, and live life free from self-destructiveness.

Sensing that there is a greater battle taking place on a spiritual plane also gives my life a deeper meaning. This is true for anyone who desires to become a spiritual warrior. Illumination from the spiritual realm confers upon me the knowledge that life is not just about learning to think and act more successfully, overcoming pesky habits, getting what I want, and feeling healthy and ready to tackle the world, but also about learning to live with integrity, love, and usefulness; not only because it will help me, but more importantly, because it will help fulfill the Divine cause of bringing love and goodness to the world.

3. Earthly terrain refers to the inner landscape upon which the warrior travels and to the circumstances in which the warrior faces inward foes. Earthly terrain concerns the difficulty of passage and the degree of opportunity for spiritual gains. It has to do with the dimension in which each battle takes place and with the measure of spiritual safety in each circumstance. It is the plane where the greater contest is ultimately played out. Within a lifetime of challenges and decisions and through a variety of external scenarios, predicaments, illusions, and revelations—mostly in the context of the mundane—the spiritual warrior fulfills the warrior role. Though the warrior is generally conscious only on one level, it is a role played out in two worlds simultaneously, of natural and spiritual life, each displaying its own changing terrain. The master warrior recognizes the ebb and flow of the battle and takes action accordingly.

The earthly terrain, thus, is the conscious, everyday world in which the warrior lives. It forms the surroundings and circumstances which the warrior faces every day. Becoming aware of the circumstances in which one lives—for example, of how one's occupation, marriage, hobbies, household, and friends affect one's spiritual being—is the way the warrior begins to take control of life. The warrior learns to distinguish between what situations cause pain or happiness and what circumstances will initiate some inward struggle or lead to peace of mind, and takes appropriate action. The master warrior doesn't sleep through life, but knows life intimately, and the terrain precisely, and walks with attention and care.

4. *Character* is a matter of wisdom and integrity, humanity, courage, and direction. It is not something inborn but rather is cultivated through spiritual combat, in both victory and defeat, for each teach their own lessons to the one who longs in humility for truth. The wise warrior is not borne of intelligence and wit on the battlefield, but of the struggle of the heart. It is love which creates wisdom, and love and wisdom joined together give birth to integrity.

The spiritual warrior is on a personal mission. This mission is as vast and comprehensive as the earthly terrain itself, and it is as high and noble as the heavenly realm. Yet the mission begins with changing not the world, but oneself. For if one battles the destructive tendencies within, the world gains a victory, the heavens gain victory, and the spiritual warrior claims the prize of victory for self.

The spiritual warrior vies against hate for the sake of love, against indifference for compassion, against cruelty for kindness, against the profane for what is sacred and holy, against what is evil for the sake of what is genuinely good. Therefore, the master warrior strives to be truly human, never raising an angry hand against an opponent, fighting only for what is right, taking up the sword of truth in defense of the neighbor, and offering the fire of love for comfort and for warmth. Therefore, the warrior challenge is of old:

> Let those who would exchange
> The life of this world for the hereafter,
> Fight for the cause of God;
> Whoever fights for the cause of God,

Whether to die or triumph
Shall be richly rewarded.
And how should you not fight . . .
For the helpless old men, women, and children
Who say, "Deliver us, Lord,
From the city of wrongdoers;
Send forth to us a guardian from Your presence;
Send to us from Your presence one who will help us"?

(Koran 4:74-75)

5. *Discipline* entails organizational effectiveness, an ability to respond to higher commands, and logistical support. Inertia, disobedience, pride, and willfulness cripple the spiritual warrior and cut off connection with spiritual allies. Making quick decisions and taking swift action according to developing circumstances, following through on orders from higher sources, and calling for support in times of need from spiritual forces in the heavenly realm are the marks of spiritual discipline.

To learn the art of discipline takes time and practice. Without practice, one cannot become an expert in anything. This is true in spiritual warfare as well. Practicing time and again to let go of self-concern and follow the Divine will, to become accustomed to giving when one would rather back away from helping others—these are ways of learning warrior discipline and control over one's self. Through such practice, one's right actions come, as it were, instinctively. They are not forced, nor contrived, but genuine offerings from a loving heart. And so we are told by Chogyam Trungpa, a wise warrior:

Warriorship is a continual journey.
To be a warrior
Is to learn to be genuine
In every moment of your life.
That is the warrior's discipline.[1]

Many spiritual warriors know something about these five criteria—the Way, the spiritual climate, the earthly terrain, character, and discipline—yet the one who seeks to understand and master them will find success in spiritual combat and take the victory, while the one who does not will not prevail. Therefore, ask yourself these questions for the sake of comparison:

> Which warrior walks more closely in the Way?
> Which warrior has the clearest grasp of the spiritual
>   climate and earthly terrain?
> Which warrior has gained the greater wisdom through
>   both victory and defeat?
> Which warrior shows more heart?
> Which warrior has mastered discipline and displays
>   obedience to principles and higher commands?
> Which warrior calls upon higher forces for aid?
> Which warrior has better instruction and training in
>   spiritual combat?

Using these criteria, it is easy to see who will win and who will lose when confronted by the spiritual foe.

If you pay attention to these assessments, taking up the challenge against inward spiritual foes will mean certain victory. If you do not pay attention to these assessments, challenging spiritual foes will be futile and mean certain defeat. You will have lost before beginning your campaign.

Knowing what can be gained from these assessments, shape a strategic advantage from them to strengthen your position. Making the most of favorable conditions will tilt the scales in your favor. You cannot win every spiritual battle, but you can win more than you lose and ultimately win the greater war for your own well-being and that of your soul.

Spiritual warfare is the art of deception, but the deception of the deceivers in the spiritual realm. When alone, act as if you are not alone. When powerful, claim no power. When in wisdom, plead ignorance. Acting as if you are by yourself while relying on the Divine, calling for power from the heavenly realm, and realizing you know nothing even though you seem to know much, are ways of defeating the spiritual foe. This is not truly deception, but paradox, causing the spiritual enemy much confusion. Yet act with care, for deception is also the greatest weapon of the spiritual foe. Where is the denial in your life? What lies are your spiritual enemies telling you that allow your self-destructive tendencies to go unchallenged?

For instance, if you are filled with righteous anger or indignation, ask yourself what right you have to judge another. What is the lie feeding that anger? If you are tempted to leave the responsibility of relationships to flee to greener pastures, ask yourself what the grand fantasy of happiness is that your spiritual enemy has set out before you. Discover the lie and you discover the truth.

If your spiritual enemy seeks some advantage entice him with it. Let him expose his true nature, for any destructive force, within or without, cannot be confronted until it is seen. Allow yourself to imagine acting on your desires, fear, lust, and rage. Imagine the effects of such an emotion in its final stages and you will see its destructive nature. Exposing the true nature of your destructive tendencies will help you defeat them, because you see them for what they really are and how devastating they can become. For instance, if you are not aware of the destructive nature of your anger, how can you deal with it? If you cannot see your selfishness, how can you give with sincerity? If you do not recognize the lust behind your love, how can you love purely? Expose your enemy! When he is exposed, attack him. However, don't tackle some defect that you know is too powerful for you to overcome until you have become fully prepared to deal with it.

The spiritual forces of destruction can truly devastate the strongest warrior, but the enemy is not wise and is often in disarray. If he is incensed, provoke him by jabs into his lines. That is, when faced with laziness, thrust yourself into action; in bouts of self-pity, force yourself to do one good thing for another. Refuse to give ground. If the enemy is rested, wear him down with new resolve. Use humility to make him haughty. Call upon a greater power to cause him to abandon the field. Attack where he is not prepared; travel by way of places where it would never occur to him you would go. These are the military strategist's calculations for spiritual victory.

The warrior who is prepared for spiritual battle even before taking the field will have the victory. One who is ill-prepared has the least strategic advantage when spiritual struggle commences. One with no preparation does not partake of the battle, having already been conquered and made prisoner. When you examine it in this way, the outcome is apparent. Therefore, know the criteria, the surroundings, and the Way, for this is the path to victory.

❋ *Further Application*

Walking In the Way

In ancient Chinese philosophy, it is said that the Way *(Tao)* that is named is not the eternal Way *(Tao)*. Therefore, any description of what the Way might be will be limited. But I think it is important for Westerners to understand the basic concept and, once it is understood, to let it grow in meaning. This understanding will only help in our spiritual quest. The Way for me is the same as the Infinite, as God, and as God's working in the world. I can relate to it in familiar Judeo-Christian terms as Providence, how the Divine provides for humankind. For me, to walk in the Way is to allow the Divine to lead and to try to enter into the gentle stream of Providence which carries all toward what is good and blessed. I know I don't naturally incline to this approach. I like to think that I can control my world and perhaps even create my own sense of happiness and well-being through forcing consequences. But the result is that I am never satisfied, and I am forever falling short in my endeavors of control. In its extreme, this predicament leads me into constant anxiety and bouts of depression. But learning to walk in the Way, by allowing God's plan to unfold the way God sees fit for my life and accepting what comes with open arms and with trust, has led to incredible inner peace. Decisions still need to be made and actions taken, but from learning trust in the Divine and acceptance, I can act from a centeredness and a calm which does not exist when I try to control the world. I can act in harmony with the Divine instead of against it, and with Providence instead of opposing it.

One way in which this principle has come into great use for me is in dealing with my teenage sons. My wife Cathy and I have four of them. Our eldest, Ronnie, now nineteen, spent the past couple of years working his way through that awkward time of wanting complete freedom without acting with complete responsibility. Parents of teens know what I am talking about. In Ron's earlier teen years, when he first began to refuse to do certain chores which he deemed below his new adult status, or would come home well past the hour he had promised, or other such infractions, I used to simply blow my top. When he was younger, I could control his actions. But this half-child, half-adult rebellion drove me crazy. I realized that my attempts at control wouldn't help him develop into a mature and independent adult. But if I didn't do anything, he'd grow up without a good sense of responsibility and would probably make some huge mistakes. As I applied this principle of walking in the Way, of allowing him to unfold and develop under God's providence, I was able to deal with his bouts of rebellion, not from anger, but from love. I grew to trust, not only in the Divine, but in my son. By learning to walk in the Way with my son, I was learning how to let go gracefully and let him grow.

One way I was able to accomplish this shift was to apply the principle that the warrior who is prepared before battle will have the victory over the one who is not. Instead of spontaneously reacting to Ron's actions with anger and a sense of loss of control, I'd do some planning ahead of time. Before he would come home late, for instance, I'd set myself some personal goals—to act from love, to trust before questioning, to stay calm, to stay firm. I would consider ahead of time which consequences would be appropriate and which would be out of order. Then, if battle did erupt upon Ron's arrival, I was ready, spiritually ready, to help him with his growth as a caring yet respectful parent. I can't say I have a perfect record, but this practice has made an incredible difference in our relationship. I am amazed at how when I react from calm, trust, and love to any adverse situation with my son, how often he will return the favor. By my endeavor to walk in the Way with him, he now endeavors to walk in the Way for himself. Teens will experiment, flare up in temperament, fabricate, take risks, and make mistakes. Everybody knows that. But a parent who gives it his or her best to act from a calm and loving base will continue to be a gentle guide on the journey and an influence for good in the young adult's life.

This principle applies not only to parenting; it is also one of the keys to healthy recovery from addiction, codependency, or any character defect from which one may be suffering. I know this personally, but have also worked with many men and women who at one time felt the world was their enemy and that life seemed to fight against them. Through alcohol and drug abuse, they would endeavor to escape the battle and perhaps gain a superficial and fleeting sense of well-being. But we know well these means are deceptive. There is a saying among alcoholics, "There is no problem a drink will not make worse." Through a program of recovery, they not only learn how to live without an artificial and temporary substitute for a sense of well-being, but they also begin a journey toward a new life which allows for a genuine and lasting sense of happiness, and even of serenity. What they are doing is learning to walk in the Way. Familiar concepts in many twelve-step programs are all means of entering this sacred path. "Surrender," "Let go and let God," "Live just for today," are all means of allowing life to unfold, of floating into that gentle stream of divine care, and of walking humbly in the Way.

Tasks

1. Sit quietly and contemplate your inner being. What motivates you and fills you with noble passion? Write a list of five good qualities with which you are blessed (e.g., benevolence, the ability to listen well, conscientiousness). What do these qualities tell you about your special gift to the world?

2. Once you have begun to discover your personal mission (it will grow and change), write down a list of the inward barriers which inhibit you from achieving that mission. These are some of your spiritual enemies.

3. Pledge to fight the good fight. Say to yourself, to your God, to the world, "Today I will act without expectation; I will fight without aggression; I will call upon a Higher Power for my aid; I will confront the forces of darkness in my life, and I will claim the victory."

Sun Tzu said:

*When you do battle, even if you are winning,
if you continue for a long time it will dull your
forces and blunt your edge; if you besiege a citadel,
your strength will be exhausted. If you keep your
armies out in the field for a long time, your supplies
will be insufficient. When your forces are dulled, your
edge is blunted, your strength is exhausted, and your
supplies are gone, then others will take advantage of
your debility and rise up. . . . Therefore, I have heard
of military operations that were clumsy but swift, but
I have never seen one that was skillful and lasted a
long time. It is never beneficial to a nation to have
a military operation continue for a long time.*

Chapter 2

The Weapons of Spiritual Warfare

The art of spiritual warfare calls for arms and supplies, since no army can expect to win without weapons or provisions for the soldiers. Similarly, no spiritual warrior can win an inward confrontation without spiritual weapons and a source of internal sustenance.

In spiritual warfare, truth is the sword which slices through the enemy shield of falsehood and deception. Truth is the sharp edge of reality, cutting away what is unreal, misleading, and fraudulent. If you seek the truth for the cause of what is noble and right, you will find it. Truth will serve you in battle, for evil has no power except in falsehood and is easily cut down with this most noble weapon.

Carry a sword which fits you well, neither too heavy and cumbersome, nor so light that it is easily broken. Do not use the sword of another, because one warrior's truth may be another's deception. Find your own weapon and treasure it as your friend and ally. Study and contemplate spiritual matters to strengthen the metal of the blade. Practice will sharpen it. Therefore, it is written of the ancient spiritual warrior:

> Gird your sword upon your thigh, O mighty one,
> With your glory and your majesty.
> And in your majesty ride prosperously
> Because of truth, humility, and righteousness;
> And your right arm shall teach you awesome things.
> (Psalm 45:3,4)

All the major religions emphasize the importance of an individual knowing the truth. Not all agree on what that truth is, but it is amazing how many religions share many of the same truths about leading a healthy spiritual life. The laws of civility exist in one form or another in most of the major religions, urging us not to live destructively. The Golden Rule to do unto others as we would want them to do unto us exists in one form or another in most religions. Truths about the blessings of trusting in the Divine, of the joy in being of service to others, of walking with integrity, abound in every religious philosophy and culture. There is no shortage of truth out there to help with one's life, and the truth we can learn about ourselves is priceless.

The teachings of all the great religions and spiritual philosophies are the arrows which will pierce the thickest armor of the dark forces. Have your quiver full of them. Their truth can puncture the most carefully crafted deceptions of the spiritual foe and can penetrate into the fears, misgivings, anger, and mistaken wants which the spiritual enemy would thrust upon each noble warrior. When these have been vanquished, they are replaced with inner serenity, consolation, safety, and peace.

The kinds of truths that have been weapons against the spiritual enemies of my life are many. These beliefs may not ring true to every warrior, and as said, the warrior must choose a sword which fits that particular warrior well, but I would like to share some of my "truths" which have helped me in battle. The truth that there is a God, and that God is a God of love, always on my side, no matter what, always reaching out to put me on the right path—what a comfort that truth has been to me! It has sliced through the self-doubt and the overwhelming sense of uselessness and lack of meaning with which the spiritual enemy would like to suffocate me. Knowing that God is always there to pick me up when I fall in battle gives me the hope and the courage to face my personal demons and the ability to get back up and try again when I fail. The truth, as the Buddha would put it, that desire is a thirst that cannot be quenched, helps me to puncture the illusion that fulfilling my desires and appetites will bring me lasting happiness. I used to believe that fulfilling my base desires would bring happiness, as I pathetically searched to find it in the abuse of drugs and alcohol, smoking, eating to excess, and other unhealthy ways. It took a lot of humiliating defeats before I learned that fulfilling these base desires does not bring lasting happiness. Through using this truth as a weapon I began to escape the claws of addiction and compulsion and to find a new way of gaining happiness through spiritual means. The truth I first heard from an elderly woman in a twelve-step meeting that, "There is a God, and it ain't me," has helped me see that my frivolous attempts to control every aspect of my world is a joke. I can't do it, and I don't have to, because I'm not God. It is God who will take care of those things beyond my control. I can let go. Hence, another meaningful truth, which I have used as a sword against many spiritual enemies that confront me over issues of anxiety, trust, and control, is the Serenity Prayer:

God, grant me the serenity
To accept the things I cannot change;
Courage to change the things I can;
And wisdom to know the difference.

As well as using truth as a sword, meditation and prayer are effective shields against harm. Learn to use them in times of strife for safety and in times of peace for comfort and stability. Through meditation the mind is stilled and focused. Communication with higher forces is established. Even in the midst of the spiritual fray, inner directives are heard and can be followed with less difficulty. Meditation helps us to become aware of what is going on around us and inside of us. It helps us hear messages that are coming to us, whether those messages be from our own body and spirit, from the world without, or from the Divine, speaking to us in the still small voice from the world within. Thich Nhat Hanh writes:

Meditation is to be aware
Of what is going on—
In our bodies,
In our feelings,
In our minds,
And in the world.[1]

Prayer is not only something to be used before the battle. It is one of the most powerful weapons during the battle. Prayer for strength, for deliverance from spiritual enemies, and for new direction in the confusion of combat is a proven means of procuring spiritual victory. Prayer is opening the way for the Divine and the spiritual forces of heaven. Prayer can call battalions of the heavenly host to fight against the legions of demons which beset the spiritual warrior. For many, prayer brings immediate answers to perplexing questions and difficult circumstances. For others, prayer provides hope and perseverance. For still others, prayer reveals a sense of divine presence and the comfort which this brings.

For me, prayer has always helped clarify whatever difficult situation I may be facing. Asking God for help, I am reminded so gently of higher truths or realities which put my life back in focus. If I am desirous of something and pray about it, I am reminded to seek God's kingdom first and all other things will come in their own time. If I am in anguish over circumstances out of my control and turn to God, I am reminded that God is in charge and that all things—even the worst—can lead to good, if we allow God to make it that way. If I am in emotional pain and pray for help, it is as if I am lifted up out of my turmoil by flights of angels, and if not immediately, then at least I sense the beginning of being lifted up and the promise of peace and healing to come. Prayer works. It is something that must be used often, with perseverance and sincerity, but it works. Lorenzo Scupoli counsels:

If you wish your prayer to bring forth much fruit,
Never be content by oral prayer alone,
But pray also with your mind and heart—

Using your mind to understand
And be conscious of all that is said in words,
And your heart to feel it all.
Above all, pray with your heart.
Prayer bursting from the heart
Is like a streak of lightning,
Which takes but a moment to cross the heavens
And appear before the throne of the all merciful God.[2]

After victory, prayers of thanks and gratitude help ensure a long and steady peace. It is a shield of defense and a true aid in spiritual combat.

Fire is also an effective tool in dispensing with spiritual foes, but it is the fire of love and not hate. The fire of love burns down the walls of denial, lays waste the weapons of destruction, and consumes intolerance and self-absorption, thus clearing away the avenues of the advancing enemy forces. The great eighteenth-century Swedish scientist and philosopher Emanuel Swedenborg wrote:

Love is spiritual fire.[3]

But love is not only a weapon against the spiritual foe. It is also a healer of wounds. It heals and gives life to those who receive it. It becomes the essence and the empowering force of the true spiritual warrior. Therefore, we are told by Chief Dan George, a wise warrior of old:

Love is something you and I must have.
We must have it because our spirit feeds upon it.
We must have it because without it we become weak
    and faint.
Without love our self-esteem weakens.
Without it our courage fails.
Without love we can no longer look out confidently at
    the world.
We turn inward and begin to feed upon our own per-
    sonalities,

And little by little we destroy ourselves.
With it we are creative.
With it we march tirelessly.
With it, and with it alone,
We are able to sacrifice for others.[4]

Weapons alone will not assure spiritual victory regardless of their number, size, effectiveness, or power, but rather the warrior's ability to call upon divine aid. It is imperative that the armies of the heavenly realm are called into service for any battle and that the warrior call upon divine help in the approaching conflict. For it is a truth that though the spiritual warrior acts as if alone, it is the Divine who fights the battle through heavenly forces, and it is the Divine who gains victory for the warrior. The one who would be a master combatant takes up the sword and fights with courage and utter determination, and yet even in the midst of the fray surrenders individual power to the Divine. In turn, the Divine empowers the warrior and grants success. This is why all great spiritual warriors know that without God they can do nothing, but with God all things are possible.

The sustenance which feeds the warrior's will is the contentment and even bliss which accompanies the spiritual path. To walk in the Way is to walk in contentment, opened to the in-flowing of spiritual energy and direction. A life determined on the course of right being and action produces much goodness and lovingkindness. These are rewarded by inward sensations of happiness and delight. The food for the warrior-soul is the delight which lovingkindness brings. It is the spiritual soldier's daily bread.

I sense this daily bread not only in my marriage and with family and friends, but also in the work I do in counseling. Helping fathers and sons reunite—or even unite for the first time through men's work—witnessing spiritual connections, along with hugs that bind them together for the first time, is exhilarating and quite nurturing to my soul. Seeing a couple, through counseling and hard work, regain faith in their marriage and begin to build a solid and loving relationship upon a foundation of commitment and mutual support has been bread enough for me for years. Witnessing a young teen regain some of the trust in people lost because of a breakup in the family and begin to feel safe to love once more is a delight that can bring tears to my eyes. The spiritual food I receive from helping others is what makes the struggles worthwhile and makes living a pleasure.

This spiritual sustenance is easier to find when things seem to be going well in the warrior's life. But in the heat of battle, things may take on a different appearance. The warrior must keep the faith and look for that which nourishes. Though in the midst of battle the supply may seem low, and hunger may ensue when involved in a prolonged campaign, the spiritual warrior is able to find enough sustenance. But care must be taken to keep supply lines open to the Source and to take in what is available at the time. This food may lack savor, but meals in the midst of war are rarely a fine banquet. It will serve until the enemy ground is taken, when supply lines can be reopened to their fullest capacity and new provisions can be gathered in peace. Whether it be a battle with fear, anger, desire, or whatever, the warrior will want to focus on the simple pleasures of life, the ones that are easily remembered and easily achieved, rather than longing for some out-of-reach state of bliss. If the warrior thinks it is all or nothing, the warrior will receive nothing. Sometimes, in order to escape an abundance of fear, one just needs to hold onto a little hope; to escape bouts of anger or rage, one needs to start with a few solid moments of peace; to escape the unquenchable thirst of desire, one may first find contentment in the simple pledge to do God's will first and above all other things. After battle, the fine banquet of spiritual bliss may emerge, but never during the fray. Look for the simple joys to get you through the rough times.

Spiritual warriors are impoverished by their own efforts when they move too far away from their Source. The greater the distance between spiritual warriors and their Source, the more they find themselves depleted of sustenance. All strength is spent on the battlefield, while inwardly, hopes and aspirations shrivel and dry up. Therefore, the master warrior never wanders far from the Source, even in the most heated battle, when the smoke of confusion rises. This means the warrior doesn't forget about God in the midst of battle, doesn't lose focus on why the particular battle is being fought, and doesn't begin to buy into the illusion that the warrior can do it without divine help. To follow these ways is to cut oneself off from the Source, and defeat becomes a certainty.

If you continue for a prolonged time in battle, even if you are winning, it will dull your inner forces and blunt your edge. In practicing spiritual battle, seek the quick victory. This has been practiced in many types of competition, especially business. Any successful business has to know when it has a valuable service or product that must be backed to the full. It does no good to market half-heartedly. It is a waste of time to market a product which has little appeal until reserves are used up. The warrior in business puts strength where strength is called for and seeks quickly to capture the market. Where the market is weak, the worthy business warrior knows when to pull out and not exhaust resources. It is the same with spiritual matters. Laying siege against an inward foe will only exhaust your strength. You cannot wait out a spiritual enemy who has taken up a walled position within your own mind. The enemy will laugh at you from his protected position, knowing he already owns a portion of your soul. You must strike swiftly and completely, with all weapons available to you. If you continue in battle for a long time, your inward reserves will not suffice. Where your forces have dulled, your edge blunted, your strength and available resources depleted, spiritual enemies will rush in from all around to take advantage of your weakness. Even with the wisest counsel, you will not be able to turn the ensuing consequences to the good. It is advisable, therefore, to seek the quick victory. If victory remains elusive, retreat to new earthly terrain and take new position on higher ground.

Dealing with one's compulsive behavior half-heartedly will not enable the warrior to gain victory over it. The compulsion will remain until a full-scale battle is waged to destroy it. Suffering from depression and emerging from its depths only from time to time to complain about how bad one feels, but not taking action to confront this devastating enemy through all the various means—such as counseling, rest, recreation, exercise, useful service—is to leave the enemy intact and the darkness and gloom in place. Just as in war between countries, all resources must be put into place to vanquish a foe. If only a half-hearted battle ensues, the battle can be excruciating and drawn out for years. Hit the enemy, no matter what it is, fast and hard, with everything you have, and if it doesn't help, move on for awhile to something else.

If one cannot find success, try giving it a rest, and come back later. Sometimes this is not possible, as, for example, when the enemy the warrior is fighting can cause immediate harm to oneself or others. But sometimes it is possible to retreat, regroup, and try again. In fact, this strategy can sometimes be just what is needed to conquer some chronic dysfunctional behavior or stubborn spiritual foe. If you engage in an all-out attack on laziness, but do not make progress, move on to something else for awhile. When you come back to it, you may find it easier to overcome. If you can't beat fear, stop trying and tackle something else. Sometimes getting away from obsessing on a particular fear often alleviates that fear in the long run. Don't get stuck in a protracted battle. If you can, move on.

Thus in war, there have been military operations that were clumsy but swift, and there have been some occasions for cleverly dragging on the hostilities, such as in modern guerilla warfare. However, this is never the case in spiritual warfare. To drag on the hostilities is to give our personal demons power, to let our dysfunctions take deeper root within our beings. To continue to half-heartedly deal with our spiritual foes is a sign that we are not serious about removing them, and we will fail to take new ground. In spiritual warfare seek the quick victory, not the protracted engagement. Thus, true master combatants are the final arbiters of their own lives and lords over the security of their own being.

❀ *Further Application*

Truth as a Weapon

I had to learn to use truth as a weapon against my spiritual adversaries. Being able to accept the truth about my shortcomings was and continues to be an incredible means of growth for me. One of my spiritual enemies is fear. The fear of death or tragedy has been a mighty adversary to my well-being. My mother, having lost a son to a sudden illness, unconsciously raised me in an aura of fear that the same thing very well might happen to me. It was so intense that every time I caught a cold as a child I thought I would most likely die. When I grew older, married, and began a family, I carried this fear into raising my own children. When my first child became ill, I'd panic. I'd reach for the thermometer and exclaim to my wife Cathy, "Oh no! He's going to die." My wife's response would seem strange to me. She'd inform me nonchalantly, "He's fine! He's got a temperature of 99. It's just a cold." It took a few years and witnessing my children's quick recovery to realize that I was suffering from a dysfunction. But it was the truth that freed me. In fact, there were many truths that sliced through the fear: the truth that I had inherited this fear from my mother and I didn't need to carry it with me; the truth that I must learn to trust in God no matter what the outcome; the truth that I had to let go; the truth that I had to stop putting this fear into my own children. All of these truths helped me to fight against the fear.

My youngest son, Steve, on the other hand, was born fearless. He has no sense of danger and would jump off the roof of our house if the other children asked him to do it. Naturally, this trait caused me some fear. One summer the family went to a religious camp outside of Pittsburgh. One of the irritating things about this camp is that while the parents attend a lecture, the children run around outside trying, no doubt, to get killed! I was worried about Steve as the lecture began, but the topic intrigued me. It was about what we unconsciously inherit from our parents. At the end of the lecture, the woman took us through a guided visualization of being a child again, in our mother's arms, and asked us to think about what our mother was saying to us. That was easy for me. She was saying, "It's a dangerous, dangerous world. Anything can happen any time." Then the woman asked us to visualize that we had an angel mother holding us. Now what was she saying? Again, it was obvious to me, "You are safe."

What that exercise brought about for me was the realization, not only of where my irrational fear of death came from, but also of how I had been putting that same fear into my children. I know that sometimes tragedy does strike and children do die, but to live in fear of this possibility is to live in the dreaded prison of this spiritual enemy. I thought to myself, "Somehow, I have to begin reversing these fears, not only with myself, but with my children. How will I ever get the opportunity to even begin with my children? How can I begin to assure them that it's a safe world? How often will the subject come up? God, help me remember this! I've got to reverse this with my children."

Not two hours later my little son Steve asked if we could go on a walk in the woods. As we walked hand and hand together down the forest path I thought of how I might introduce the subject, but it just didn't seem to be that easy. Then, at once, he stopped me on the path, looked at me with bright, alert eyes, and asked if he could tell me something. He said, "You know something Dad? I haven't died yet." Astonished and overjoyed, I looked into his eyes, and said, "You know something son, it's hard to die." I then cocked my head toward the heavens and whispered, "Thanks."

Tasks

1. *In a state of peaceful contemplation ask yourself, "What do I know to be true about my life?" (For instance, I myself know that when I am loving I am happier, that when I work too hard I lose touch with my spirituality, and that my tendency toward excess can get me into trouble.) Write down what you observe. Determine how this knowledge can help you in your spiritual struggles.*

2. *Begin the day with a quiet time of prayer and meditation. In your prayers, ask only for the wisdom needed for this day, and in your meditation, listen for answers. Note how this quiet time impacts your day.*

3. *Procure an ancient text of wisdom, such as the Bible, the Koran, the Tao Te Ching, or some other sacred book. Read only a small portion each night before retiring. Read it with a desire to learn something for life. Note what it teaches you.*

Sun Tzu said:

The general rule for use of the military is that it is better to keep a nation intact than to destroy it. It is better to keep an army intact than to destroy it, better to keep a division intact than to destroy it, better to keep a battalion intact than to destroy it, better to keep a unit intact than to destroy it. Therefore those who win every battle are not really skillful—those who render others' armies helpless without fighting are the best of all. . . .

CHAPTER 3

Combat Strategy

Sun Tzu says that the general rule of military strategy is that it is better to keep an army intact than to destroy it. To win a hundred victories in a hundred battles is not the highest excellence; the highest excellence is to subdue the enemy without fighting at all.

The same is possible in spiritual warfare—to subdue the enemy's forces without going to battle, to take the enemy without an attack, and to crush the enemy's state without a protracted campaign. Some destructive tendencies can, under certain circumstances, be overcome without struggle. However, this outcome calls for total submission to the divine will and surrender to the Way. By assessing the enemy and maneuvering into a position of clear superiority, the enemy may lose heart and retreat without a fight. The master warrior is capable of turning self-will over to the Divine in such a way that the enemy recognizes the futility of confrontation and so retreats. In order to accomplish this result, the spiritual warrior must concentrate on the following precepts:

> Submit *unconditionally* to the divine will.
> Be willing to follow new commands that may seem to
>   go against natural instinct.
> Take up positions on the earthly terrain which are virtu-
>   ally impregnable to the opponent.
> Allow for new and unfamiliar forces to take the field
>   and command the impending battle.

In submitting to the divine will, the master warrior receives new strength and guidance. Through challenging old habits and natural instincts, the master warrior learns new patterns of living, takes the higher ground, and finds support from heavenly forces who join the battle against the spiritual opponents. This is tantamount to winning by means of the Way (*Tao*), and it is generally only accomplished by the great masters of spiritual warfare. Most spiritual warriors have too much self-will to relinquish command, and not enough trust to rely on the Divine. Furthermore, fear of the unknown may cause a novice warrior to engage in a particular battle alone rather than rely on unfamiliar allies, regardless of their helpful disposition, strength, and spiritual origin.

I personally have witnessed this unconditional surrender to the Divine—and thus complete and total victory without a protracted battle—in those who have given up addiction in favor of a twelve-step program. For many, the life change is dramatic. Having given up substance abuse, their path of surrender is complete and total. They come to know that there are no compromises in escaping addiction, no prodding the enemy lines a bit here and a bit there to detect weaknesses while continuing to drink or abuse drugs. In order to obtain wholeness and sobriety, there must be an immediate change in life style, with a complete turning of one's life over to the care of God. Many who struggled unsuccessfully to quit on their own found that when they were finally able to submit completely to the divine will, and allow a higher power to guide them, their struggle disappeared instantaneously. What seemed so painfully impossible became a reality. They become free of addiction, and, for some, it even feels as if they have been, in traditional Christian terms, "saved" from their addiction. This subduing of an old, familiar, and powerful enemy is followed up by taking positions on earthly terrain which are impenetrable. That is, they no longer hang out at the bars, or associate with friends who may lead them back into their drinking. They form alliances in support groups and friendships with those who will help them stay victorious. This type of victory, which is instantaneous, bloodless, and enduring, really can take place with those who are serious about their spiritual growth. Furthermore, victory doesn't only occur with those who take up arms against addiction, but can take place against any spiritual foe, if one is serious, committed, and ready to rely on the power of the Divine and the support of others.

After winning many hard-fought battles and strengthening one's own spiritual forces through such victories, the veteran warrior will become more easily disposed to such a strategy and find it more and more possible to win without a confrontation. This, then, is the goal: the true champion of spiritual warfare wins the battle without entering into the battle.

> When one sets aside desires,
> All that have entered the mind . . .
> And is contented in self and through self,
> That person is said to be one of steady wisdom.
>
> The one whose mind stirs not in sorrows,
> Who in joys longs not for joys,
> The one whose passion, fear, and wrath are gone,
> That steady-minded one is called a sage.
> (Bhagavad Gita 2:55-56)

The one who journeys to lasting peace endures many battles along the way. Through victory in inward temptation and struggle, spiritual peace is achieved. When battle must ensue, here is the art of using your resources:

When you sense that you are much stronger than your inward spiritual foe, surround him and attack him; when you and the enemy are equally matched, divide him; when you are inferior in strength, take the defensive; and when you are no match for the enemy, avoid him. You surround a spiritual enemy by deploying your resources fully to the challenge at hand. To attack is to move forward in strong opposition, using those resources to capacity. For instance, you know you have a bad habit that you can beat. Perhaps this habit is simply interrupting people in conversation, or occasionally using inappropriate language, or maybe it's slipping into gossiping about others. Knowing this spiritual enemy is small and seemingly insignificant, it is still important to surround it and attack it with full force. Half-hearted measures will fail, even with the most insignificant shortcomings. Take them all seriously and give them your full attention and effort. Make a promise to yourself that you will work on beating this habit until it is gone. Write yourself a note and set in on your dresser, or keep it in your shirt pocket, to remind yourself that you are serious about this battle. Pray to God to remove it from you, even though it seems insignificant. Ask for help from others you trust to call you on your misbehavior. These are some ingredients to a full-out attack. To engage the spiritual enemy is to poke and prod his lines in search of weaknesses in his battle array. To avoid a superior enemy is to flee from his presence and escape certain defeat.

Fleeing from the enemy does not mean succumbing to one's destructive tendencies, or giving up on one's efforts to subdue base desires and wants. On the contrary, it means that if certain circumstances needlessly throw the warrior into a battle that cannot be won, then the warrior should flee. It is not the mark of an intelligent warrior to remain in such circumstances, fighting only to lose again and again.

For example, one must avoid circumstances that lead to instant bouts of anger or rage. A parent who continually loses the battle against controlling anger when his or her four year old throws a tantrum must get help, either through the spouse or others. The situation is too dangerous to act alone, especially if one's anger has turned to violence. A man suffering from alcoholism must avoid the bar scene, no matter how many friends he will miss from not being there. The stakes are too high. For another example, if faced with a repeating scenario which causes one to lose the war over lust, then change the scenario. For a man or woman who is trying to escape from addiction to sex or relationships, coffee with available members of the opposite sex becomes out of the question. Some deeper levels of intimate friendship become off limits, especially if these were paths to acting out the addiction. Lastly, if one finds that certain situations inevitably activate feelings of self-pity and depression, then avoid those situations. Perhaps sitting in front of the computer for a few hours each night, isolated from others, is the trap. Or maybe it's lying in bed too long in the morning and listing all the challenges that must be faced that day may bring on instant burdens that do not need to be carried.

Flee from all such scenarios. They help make our problems even worse, or may even cause them. Do not remain in circumstances where you regularly and continually lose your battle against your spiritual enemy. Retreat! This approach isn't a complicated formula, but it is often overlooked by the average warrior, who continues to fight and lose in circumstances which could be altogether avoided. The master warrior recognizes when battles do not need to be fought at all and avoids those which most likely will end in defeat.

The spiritual warrior's decision-making ability is the guardian of the soul. When this guard is in place, the soul will certainly be safe; when it is defective, the soul will certainly be in peril. The master warrior makes military decisions based upon rational wisdom, love for others, and humility. The questions one must ask oneself are: What good or ill will this decision bring? Is it necessary? For whom and for what purpose is this decision made? For example, employers who act from spiritual principles do not base their decisions on profit alone, but take into consideration the needs and welfare of the employees, as well. Spiritually-minded executives care about the impact of what they do, create, or provide with respect not only to the bottom line, but also to the customer's welfare, the environment, and the long-term benefit to society. One who makes decisions based on profit alone may gain the whole world, as Jesus said, but loses his or her own soul in the process. In spiritual warfare, the decision to take a certain path, to fight or not to fight, is not about personal gain and glory, but for the sake of the greater good, and in obedience and allegiance to the divine will and command. As Carlos Castaneda writes:

> A warrior must always keep in mind
> That a path is only a path. . . .
> His decision to keep on that path
> Or to leave it
> Must be free of fear and ambition.
> He must look at every path closely and deliberately.
> There is a question that a warrior has to ask:
> Does this path have a heart?[1]

There are three ways in which a faulty decision-making process can bring grief to the spiritual warrior:

> To decide to advance against a spiritual foe, not realizing that one is in no disposition to do so, or to begin a retreat, not realizing that one is in no position to withdraw—this is defeating one's self.
> To go into battle without a strong connection to the Source and the help of spiritual allies.
> To fight for reasons other than those which are noble, such as self-promotion, honor, glory, or gain. In this case, a new enemy secretly joins your ranks, only to turn on you when in the heat of the battle. This is called sowing disorder in your own ranks and handing over the victory.

To advance prematurely against a spiritual foe is to confront some destructive tendency in one's life when one is not emotionally prepared to do so. For instance, someone who suffers from an unhealthy relationship that needs to be broken off, but who has not prepared himself for the sense of loss he will encounter, is entering the battle prematurely. Most likely that person will return to the unhealthy relationship in no better, or perhaps even worse shape, but now at the mercy of the other party and feeling totally defeated. On the other hand, getting involved in a serious love relationship immediately after breaking up from a long-term relationship is also self-defeating, for healing has not yet taken place, lessons have not been learned, and a healthy degree of independence has not been achieved.

To go into battle without a strong connection to the Source is threatening to one's self-integrity. Often when people suffer from depression, especially men, they are reluctant to share with others the anguish they are experiencing. They do not want to be judged or seen as inadequate, so they struggle in isolation. Their chances of defeating this enemy alone are slim. They need to reach out for help. The average warrior only calls on God or other people when circumstances seem to indicate no other way. The master warrior, however, calls on God in every battle and relies on allies whenever they are present.

To fight against personal demons for ignoble reasons—such as to modify behavior for personal gain or to deceive others—is the mark not only of a foolish warrior, but of a charlatan and a spiritual fraud, for it is not really a fight but a masking of intentions. Moreover, to fight against one's personal demons for one's own peace of mind is not trickery, but neither is it the highest excellence, for one still acts from selfish motives and hands over the victory to a stronger foe—selfishness itself. On the other hand, the one who struggles with what is destructive and hurtful in one's self, for the sake of self and others, does so from a spiritual motivation. One who fights for the sake of the Divine can be called a saint. Castaneda observes:

> The average man acts
> Only if there is the chance for profit.
> Warriors act not for profit,
> But for the spirit.[2]

Taking all that has been said into account, there emerge five factors in determining what kind of spiritual warrior will win the battle against the inner foe:

> The warrior who knows when to fight and when not to
> fight will take the victory.
> The warrior who understands how to deal with superior
> strength and inferiority in the deployment of
> force and resources will take the victory.
> The warrior whose purpose is to fulfill the divine will
> shall take the victory.
> The warrior who follows a fully prepared strategy when
> engaged in spiritual combat will take the victory.
> The warrior with sound decision-making ability in the
> art of spiritual warfare will take the victory.

These five factors are the way of anticipating victory. As Sun Tzu says:

> If you know the enemy and yourself
> You will never be at risk in a hundred battles;
> If you do not know the enemy but know yourself
> You will sometimes win and sometimes lose;
> If you know neither the enemy nor yourself
> You will be at risk in every battle.

Therefore, explore the self. Discover the spiritual enemies which hold you in captivity and surprise you at every turn, attacking your peace of mind and well-being, bringing you pain, and sowing dissension into the ranks of your inward thoughts and meditations. Study these enemies. Know them well. And when you study them closely, recognize how you yourself, your conscious self, reacts to such impulses, to the oppression, the attacks, the subtle discrepancies to what you know is good and useful. Study yourself. Know yourself well. If you know these things and rely on the Source to guide you, you cannot lose.

❋ *Further Application*

Subduing the Enemy Without Fighting

Sun Tzu said: to win a hundred victories in a hundred battles is not the highest excellence; the highest excellence is to subdue the enemy without fighting at all. This advice not only saves bloodshed in potential military confrontations, but when used as a spiritual principle, can save a person from so much pain and grief in spiritual conflict. The principle is clear: If you can avoid a situation where you're going to be thrust into spiritual strife, then by all means do so. You don't have to fight every battle. I have talked to recovering alcoholics who have time and again spent their early days of recovery trying to survive hanging with the same bar crowd and staying sober at the same time. They thrust themselves into a needless inner battle between their new selves and their old addictive selves. Most learned very quickly that this was a needless battle to keep their newly cherished recovery. It wasn't worth fighting a hundred battles to stay sober, when they could avoid the fight altogether by changing their social habits. In this way they could win by not fighting at all.

A question anyone on the path to spiritual growth can ask is, "What battles am I fighting that I don't need to fight in order to win?" One mother spoke about her dilemma with trying to wake up her teenage son for school. Both of them suffered from severe bouts of grumpiness in the morning, and they would end up fighting over breakfast and putting a damper on the whole day. She wanted to know what she could do about her anger in this situation and how she could stop it from affecting their relationship so deeply. She was tired of the battle to wake him up and tired of the constant struggle with her own anger. Rather than attempting to help her tackle this particular challenge with anger, I asked her the question. Did she even have to fight that battle? Why not have her husband wake the boy up and avoid the whole ugly mess? To do this meant that the boy had to rise fifteen minutes earlier, but as it turned out, he responded to Dad's voice at his door in a much more congenial and responsive manner than he did to Mom's, and that particular problem was solved very quickly. With this battle won without fighting at all, she could then focus on other aspects of her life where she desired improvement. Her energy level sky-rocketed, and her relationship with her son improved dramatically without any battle.

I used this principle at work. Three years ago I moved into a pleasant office that was very quiet and private. The mornings were nice, for my assistant and some other workers cheered the halls outside my door, and I energetically tackled the tasks before me. But in the afternoon, when the help was gone, the whole wing was empty and silent. I'd rarely see or hear anyone. For some, that might be heaven. For me, it became a challenge. I'd find that after three o'clock my energy was waning. Having no one around for mental or social stimulation, or to keep me accountable, I'd find myself struggling to get anything done. I'd sit there in front of the computer staring, wondering how to motivate myself with all this privacy. I strained to get anything accomplished and felt extremely guilty about it. Then it hit me that I was fighting a battle I didn't need to fight. Instead of toughing it out late afternoons, I started changing my morning meetings to the late afternoon and inquired if any of the staff wanted to work afternoons instead of mornings. It turned out that this worked better for one staff member, and though not every afternoon is filled with people and meetings, it's much more lively, and I find I have energy again. Consequently, I have even found more energy in the few days that the wing is still empty, because I have brought a certain balance to my life in this regard. Instead of fighting this nagging battle, I found a way to win without fighting at all.

Tasks

1. Practice nonreaction. When confronted with a situation where you might instinctively react with destructive thoughts or actions (for example, someone insults you), take a mental step backward and simply observe. Notice what thoughts and feelings pass in and out of consciousness. Notice that you do not have to react destructively. In freedom, choose a constructive reaction.

2. When in bouts of frustration and a desire to control what is uncontrollable, pray and meditate on these words, "God, not my will, but Thy will be done."

3. Enlist aid from spiritual allies. Call upon the Divine in times of battle to send help. For it is written of old, "He will give his angels charge over you, to keep you in all your ways" (Psalm 91:11).

Sun Tzu said:

*In ancient times skillful warriors first
made themselves invincible and then watched for
vulnerability in their opponents . . . . Invincibility is a
matter of defense; vulnerability is a matter of attack.
Defense is proper for times of insufficiency; attack
for times of surplus. Those skilled in defense hide
in the deepest depths of the earth, whereas those
skilled in attack maneuver in the heights of the
sky. Therefore, they can preserve themselves
and achieve complete victory.*

CHAPTER 4

Strategic Dispostions

*I*n ancient times, great warriors practiced the art of making themselves invincible and then waited for enemies to expose their vulnerability. One can become invincible, but one cannot guarantee the vulnerability of a spiritual enemy. That is why it is of the utmost importance that the spiritual warrior focus on the self, become strong in areas that are weak, seek health where there is spiritual sickness, and build upon the moral and spiritual strengths which already exist within. In this way, victory can be anticipated, although it cannot be forced.

Becoming invincible is a matter of learning to defend oneself from the onslaught of spiritual enemies, being able to repel destructive impulses, discriminate truth from lies, and ward off the influence of dark forces. If one assumes a defensive posture, it is because the spiritual enemy's strength is overwhelming; if one launches the attack, it is because the spiritual enemy's strength is deficient.

The expert at spiritual defense remains firmly planted in the deepest recesses of the earth, becoming one with the ground, virtually invisible and unmovable, yet aware. The warrior firmly establishes a position of inward strength which acts as a shield against the attack of spiritual foes. This tactic is accomplished by learning the art of awareness and control. The master warrior studies the inward terrain of the self through the practice of constant self-awareness. The expert at defense moves with awareness across this terrain, observing with distance and precision. Even when preoccupied by matters of the mundane, the inward eye remains sharply focused on the spiritual horizon, ready for an approaching enemy.

This is the way that leads to an awakening of spirit from the numbness of spiritual sleep. No longer associating with personal ego, the master warrior steps aside and observes. Like a child exploring the sky at midday, the master of defense learns to watch inward thoughts and emotions pass by like so many clouds in the sky. The master warrior does not reach out to grab hold of them, professing, "I own this one, or that!" The master warrior does not point to one and exclaim, "This one is me." The expert in spiritual defense does not grasp the thoughts of the mind and the emotions of the will as one's own self, but only observes. In this way, the enemy cannot approach, for there is no cover for his approach and no clear target for attack. In the *Tao Te Ching*, Lao Tzu advises:

> Empty your mind of all thoughts.
> Let your heart be at peace.
> Watch the turmoil of beings,
> But contemplate their return. . . .
> If you don't realize the source,
> You stumble in confusion and sorrow.[1]

Experts at spiritual defense become grounded through control of their emotions, thoughts, and actions. They do not wait for the enemy to move against them and *then* plan their defense. Through self-discipline and meditation, reaction to attack is instantaneous, striking as the enemy raises his weapon. Experts strike because they anticipate. They anticipate because they see. They see because they are awake. They are awake because they have taken a position outside of the sleeping self.

There is no excuse for becoming a victim of one's own negative feelings, even if they are triggered by others. Warriors who gain control over their lives recognize the destructive thoughts and feelings which attack them—the anger and resentment, the self-pity, the fear and anxiety—and they separate their conscious selves from these negative impulses. Instead of reacting to outward circumstances from impulsive emotions, the master warrior acts from inner strength. This is the essence of meditation, to become aware of one's thoughts and feelings as they flow into one's consciousness, not identifying with any of them, but allowing them to float away. One cannot do this with every thought and feeling, because the goal is not to become devoid of thoughts and feelings. But the master warrior, through practice in nonidentification with thoughts and feelings, gains control over them.

To practice the art of defense, find a time and place for meditation. Stand firmly on the earth and allow its peace to rise up into your body and soothe you. Sense the strength of Mother Earth and her centeredness. Invite it into your heart and being. Raise your hands to the sky, greet the sun, and call in the light of heaven. Imagine it entering your body, becoming one with the feeling of peace you have received from the earth. In this peaceful state, imagine a safe and sacred place, perhaps a place you visited as a child, a place where you would go for comfort. If you cannot think of one, create one. What do the surroundings look like? What colors do you see there? What does it smell like? Are there special animals there? A favorite pet? Birds? What kind? Invite those people you love and trust into this space, those whom you can imagine supporting you in difficult times. Invite God, as you understand God, into this space. Feel yourself surrounded by love, peace, safety. Meditate on this space often, and allow it to become as real as possible.

When you find yourself under attack by negative thoughts or feelings—perhaps you are in an argument—go to this place in your mind and let yourself be surrounded by the ones you love. It will help you stay peaceful and not simply react. If you find yourself worrying about some situation and begin to lose your trust in God, letting fearful feelings and their accompanying thoughts attack you, go to this safe place in your imagination. Let it be real; observe the thoughts and feeling from this place. It will make a difference. If you can create a safe place in your imagination, you are giving yourself a buffer from simply accepting negativity into your life. You give yourself a chance to react rationally to your problems, rather than on impulse. You have a chance to exercise freedom and control. This is one method of establishing yourself in the earth and becoming a master of defense.

The master of the spiritual attack, on the other hand, strikes from out of the highest reaches of the heavens. This warrior fights for the sake of what is higher and nobler than self. Thus the expert on the attack is able both to protect self and to achieve complete victory. Such an attack is launched when the enemy shows clear vulnerability. When weakness is perceived in the spiritual foe, the master warrior strikes like lightning from above. Through striking quickly, the victory is achieved, since thereby the inward foe is prevented from strengthening forces and taking a foothold. This is what can be accomplished through immediate action.

An offensive campaign against the spiritual aggressors within calls for a series of sequential actions to be followed through with precision. There are several means of spiritual assault which must be put into place. The factors in the art of spiritual combat are fivefold: self-examination, assessment of one's spiritual condition, the solicitation of divine assistance, right action, and victory. The earthly terrain gives rise to self-examination; self-examination gives rise to assessment; assessment gives rise to solicitation; solicitation gives rise to right action; right action gives rise to victory. When a spiritual warrior discovers, through careful self-scutiny, a stronghold of the inward foe, and upon determining the exact nature of the situation, calls for divine aid in routing the enemy forces and then proceeds to attack, victory is procured. This is spiritual combat. Swedenborg observes:

> The root of evil is not removed,
> Except through combat.[2]

Assuming a defensive posture protects one from defeat, whereas taking up the offense against inward foes assures victory. One who takes up this offensive campaign studies the self in order to discover where the enemy may be hiding. The warrior on the offensive looks for destructive tendencies, bad habits, or evil and deceitful ways that may have gone unnoticed within the warrior's life and being. In the Twelve Step program, this is called making a searching and fearless moral inventory of one's self, whereas in other spiritual disciplines it is called self-examination or self-observation. The first step in the attack is to look honestly at one's self and see where one falls short of integrity and impeccability. Thus Chogyam Trungpa, the master warrior, urges us to look hard at ourselves:

How often have you turned away,
Because you feared you might discover
Something terrible in yourself?
How often have you been willing
To look at your face in a mirror,
Without being embarrassed?
How many times have you tried to shield yourself
By reading the newspaper, watching television,
or just spacing out?

That is the sixty-four-thousand-dollar question:
How much have you connected with yourself
at all in your whole life?[3]

Once the master warrior has discovered the enemy, whether it be laziness or self-centeredness, desire or lust, or hidden anger or resentment, the master warrior assesses how this particular enemy can be ejected from his or her life. For example, the warrior assesses the strength of, say, resentment. Can it be moved? What steps need to be taken to crush this enemy and replace it with forgiveness and understanding? After having made such assessments, the master warrior brings it before the Divine and takes counsel, asking for specific help in dealing with this foe. The master knows that no spiritual enemy is removed without divine aid and that the roots of anger and resentment can grow deep. After soliciting such help, the warrior attacks. This attack comes by consciously changing one's behavior, letting go of resentment, praying for and receiving compassion for others, and experiencing forgiveness. The battle continues, sometimes for many years, before the warrior recognizes that progress is being made. Victory is achieved when the resentment, or whatever the spiritual enemy may be, has been vanquished and ejected for the life of the master warrior.

Though this may seem a paradox, lightning actions of this type of offensive campaign are nonactions. The choice not to follow through with destructive thoughts or desires, not to act impulsively from animal instinct, combined with the choice to act courageously for the sake of something higher than self-fulfillment or bodily pleasure, are means of assault on the spiritual foe within. More often than not, nonaction is action in the battle of the spirit. More often than not, nonaggression on the earthly terrain is full frontal assault on the forces of darkness in the spiritual realm. This is because to stop doing evil is to do good. Thich Nhat Hanh comments:

> Sometimes if we don't do anything,
> We help more than if we do a lot.[4]

To experience a victory over some destructive tendency within oneself does not necessarily call for great skill. Winning inward battles for one's own peace of mind is not necessarily the mark of a spiritual champion. It is not the highest excellence. Even to win the battle against some obvious character defect, so that the whole world gives praise, is not the highest excellence. To lift an autumn leaf is no mark of strength; to observe the sun, moon, and stars is no mark of clear sight; to hear a thunder clap is no mark of keen hearing. To glory in spiritual victory is not the mark of an expert spiritual combatant. The young spiritual warrior who desires glory by seeking a mighty foe with which to do battle is a fool and will soon discover the folly of such ambition in humiliating defeat. Those whom the ancients called experts in spiritual battle gained victory where victory was easily gained. Ancient master combatants were not victorious through incredible cleverness or through boundless courage. Rather, ancient master combatants made no mistakes. Making no mistakes means to act where victory is certain and to conquer an enemy that has already lost. This is the ideal to strive for. Thus it is said of old, "You shall be perfect, just as your Father in heaven is perfect" (Matthew 5:48).

Therefore, the expert in spiritual battle takes a stand on ground that is unassailable and does not miss the chance to defeat an enemy. For this reason, the master warrior only enters battle after having first won the victory, while the defeated warrior only seeks victory after having first entered the fray. It is a matter of right disposition. To prepare oneself for confrontation with the inward foe; to have a plan of attack and to act upon it; to give every ounce of strength in order to defeat the enemy, all the while pleading for higher aid, panting for victory for no other reason than for the sake of spiritual peace—this is the mark of the champion. One who is practiced at achieving superiority over the spiritual enemy creates opportunity for victory in this way, and therefore avoids defeat.

It is of no surprise, therefore, that the way of the ancient warrior includes basic principles of right disposition. With such a constitution, the spiritual warrior becomes able to repel spiritual assaults and to attack spiritual enemies at will, from inward discernment, integrity, and fortitude. As described by Taisen Deshimaru, there are the seven essential principles of the samurai warrior, which also apply to every spiritual warrior:

> *Gi:* the right decision, made with equanimity;
>> the right attitude; the truth. When we die,
>> we must die. Rectitude.
> *Yu:* bravery tinged with heroism.

55

Jin: universal love; benevolence toward humankind;
    compassion.
Rei: right action—a most essential quality; courtesy.
Makoto: utter sincerity; truthfulness.
Melyo: honor and glory.
Chugo: devotion; loyalty.[5]

It is through a combination of these principles that the
warrior is able to stand ground against enemies, to take necessary aggressive action, and to know the value and difference
between these alternatives. Through expert decision making
based upon spiritual values, honesty toward oneself and others,
and devotion to a noble cause, the spiritual warrior makes no
mistakes. Through right action—the kind of action which risks
personal loss for greater spiritual gain, is motivated by compassion for others, and is taken for the sake of a divine cause—
the expert in spiritual combat moves the enemy with ease.
Thus, the expert is able to be the arbiter of victory and defeat.

Through the right disposition, a victorious warrior comes
against spiritual enemies like the thrust of a hundred pounds
against the force of a few ounces. Such a warrior fights with
the power of the angels as companions in battle. On the other
hand, a defeated warrior, one who does not cultivate a spiritual
disposition of strength, fights as if pitting a few ounces against
the force of a hundred pounds. This warrior, standing alone,
falls immediately when put to the moral or spiritual test. It
is through cultivating a spiritual disposition that the master
warrior carries the full weight of victory. The power of launch-
ing into battle with the right disposition can be compared
to an immense river of cascading water thundering through
a steep canyon. What can stop it? How will it not reach
its destination?

❋ Further Application

The Art of Awareness and Control

The spiritual warrior who firmly establishes a position of inward strength shields the attack of spiritual foes. This advantage is accomplished by learning the art of awareness and control. We don't have to be victims of our own negative feelings, even if they are triggered by others. We can have control of our lives, if we can recognize the negative thoughts and feelings which attack us and separate ourselves from them. Instead of reacting to outward circumstances from impulsive emotions, we can act from inner strength.

I know I have buttons people can push which tend to trigger all sorts of destructive thoughts and feelings. When people criticize my professional integrity because they don't agree with my philosophy of ministry, I can become irate. How dare they judge me! When I feel rejected, in any situation, whether it involves being turned down on a proposal, or snubbed by one of my teenage boys, or put off by my spouse or a friend, I can feel like a little lost boy in the middle of an empty canyon, crying for Mommy. There are other buttons as well which can send me into a funk or frenzy. For most of my life, it would just happen uncontrollably. But I have made incredible progress using this principle of staying centered in inward strength and not associating with those negative feelings. I can't say I'm perfect, but I don't automatically react to external negative input. I observe. I sense the feelings inside me and see the thoughts associated with them before I adopt them as "my own." They rise up like an enemy reconnaissance patrol over the horizon, poking and prodding my lines of defense for weak spots, looking for a way in. Sometimes they do sneak in. But much of the time I choose whether to adopt them into my conscious mind and actions, and more often than not, I reject them and send them back to their enemy camp. This is very different from the old days when an inward button would be pushed and ten thousand battalions of negative thoughts and emotions would sweep into my unfortified consciousness and wreak havoc with my soul.

The way I learned to make this change was through a combination of techniques. The first was to come to the real awareness that I am not my thoughts and emotions, but rather the one who chooses them. This was made clear to me through a very simple story told me once by a very wise man. He told me to imagine I am driving behind a car which is traveling way below the speed limit. How do I feel? Angry, of course. This jerk should pull off the road if he can't drive the speed limit! Now the car comes to an intersection and slams into the car in front of it. How do I feel witnessing this? Alarmed, I suppose, but maybe even more angry that this stupid idiot hit the car in front of him. Then I get out of my car to rush up to the man in the car in front of me and hear someone say, "He's had a heart attack!" Besides feeling more alarm, perhaps in the back of my mind I am sorry I was angry at him for his slow driving. I then look into the car and see the man collapsed behind the wheel. It is my father! How do I feel? I am in tears and in terror. Look at all those different emotions in those varying circumstances. From anger to terror, I've run the gambit in this exercise. Now, anyone would have a severe reaction to see a loved one in peril. But what about being angry at that slow driver before I knew it was my father? Did I have to be angry or did I choose the anger? Was there really cause for anger, now knowing who the driver was? Should knowing the driver make a difference in how I react? Could I have reacted to the slow driver differently from the beginning? The point is, I chose my initial angry reaction, based on a set of assumptions that turned out to be wrong. I didn't *have* to react to the slow driver with anger. People can't *make* me feel happy, angry, sad, or even fearful. I *choose* these emotions based on my perceptions. And if I observe the thoughts and feelings coming to me in any situation, I can choose to modify them, reject them, or do whatever I want. If I recognize I am not the thoughts or feelings but the one who chooses them, I begin to take control of them rather than allowing them to control me. Now, when I sense myself growing impatient driving behind a slow poke, I say to myself, "That could be someone I love," and decide to let the anger pass.

It is also important for me to stay centered in the Source, who for me is God. Meditation is a good practice in allowing room for healing and peaceful thoughts to flow in from a higher Source. Meditation also gives me time to center on what is truly important in my life—my relationship with God, my desire for integrity, my ability to rise above petty thoughts and negative feelings. But more than this, I have come into the practice of calling God into my life in times when I know my buttons may be pushed. I ask God to keep me feeling whole, to remain conscious and conscientious in dealing with others. As Robert Moore would say, I try to stay in my "king energy," which for me means consciously acting and even reacting from a God-centered disposition, with calmness and a sense of the divine royalty of God protecting and guiding me.

I know these principles have helped a friend of mine a great deal in his struggle to live with a partner who, in childhood, was severely sexually abused. We know the horrendous damage that is done to young women and men who have suffered at the cruel hands of others, and how it can have a devastating effect on every aspect of a person's life. I have come to appreciate how difficult it can also be, at times, for the spouse of a victim to cope with the tragic results of such abuse, which often manifests itself in extreme dysfunctional behavior. As my friend worked with his wife through the hell of recurring memories, bouts of suicidal depression, fits of rage, and emotional absence, he confided that, "If I did not learn to set aside my instinctive reactions, I wouldn't survive. She needs me, my love and my support. I know the rage isn't about me. I know the times when nothing on this earth that I could do or say to make her feel better are not my fault. I don't let those thoughts in. I don't need them. I just hold her, if she'll let me. I love her so much I just ask God to give me the strength to be there for her." I salute this spiritual warrior for his dedication and love and for the spiritual discipline of remaining firmly implanted in the earth, centered in the Creator, awake and aware, so that he may be of help to the one he loves and who needs his love so much.

Tasks

1. Practice the following meditation. Find a safe and quiet place where you will not be disturbed. Sit or lay down in a comfortable position. Practice emptying your mind of thoughts by not holding onto them as they float into consciousness. Watch them float in and out of your mind, allowing your mind to empty itself. Continue this process for at least a half-hour. Repeat this process each day. Notice the peace and self-control you gain from it. Remember, this type of meditation is a discipline to be learned and practiced. The more you practice it, the more beneficial the results.

2. Make a brief assessment of your spiritual condition. Set aside a time with pencil and paper to take a personal moral inventory of both your constructive and destructive tendencies, your negative and positive attributes, and your spiritual strengths and weaknesses.

Also consider what you would like to change about yourself. Be honest and be fair with yourself during this process. What do you see and learn?

3. *If you feel you are ready, choose a destructive tendency with which to do battle. If this process is new to you, choose something minor (a bad habit, negative thought pattern, etc.). Examine its strengths and vulnerabilities, noticing when and where it is strong and when and where it is weak. Discover and admit your part in allowing it to rule over you. Sincerely call upon the divine power to rid this from your life. Consciously choose nonaction in battling it. Do not act upon it. It will struggle to conquer you, but if you stand your ground in nonaction, it will weaken and retreat. You will experience victory over that spiritual enemy.*

Sun Tzu said:

Governing a large number as though governing a small number is a matter of division into groups. Battling a large number as though battling a small number is a matter of forms and calls. Making the armies able to take on opponents without being defeated is a matter of unorthodox and orthodox methods. For the impact of armed forces to be like stones thrown on eggs is a matter of emptiness and fullness.

CHAPTER 5

Creating Spiritual Advantage

*I*n general, it is organization that makes managing many challenges the same as managing a few. It is a matter of dividing the challenges into groups and dealing with each as a separate yet related issue. No one can stand against one hundred spiritual enemies, but one can confront the weakest of the one hundred and consequently defeat them all. Battling a large number of spiritual foes as though battling a small number is a matter of maneuvering and communication with the Divine. Through maneuvering one can throw great force against a strong spiritual enemy, attacking where the enemy is weak and maneuvering where the enemy does not expect. Through communication with the Divine, the force one exerts can become boundless.

Any spiritual warrior can fight without losing. It is a matter of using the unorthodox and orthodox methods. Knowing the distinction between weak and strong points in the spiritual enemy makes one's inner forces fall upon the enemy like hurling a stone into a basket of eggs.

In battle, confrontation is done directly and victory is gained by using the element of surprise. The unorthodox method creates the element of surprise because it makes the warrior unpredictable, and the spiritual enemy is then left guessing every move. Therefore, those skilled at the unorthodox are as boundless as the heavens and earth and as inexhaustible as the great rivers and seas.

Using the orthodox method entails striking the enemy directly with all the power the warrior can gather. This tactic can be accomplished by refusing to fight against those inner destructive forces which are too powerful to be dealt with efficiently and challenging the weaker powers instead. That is, the wise warrior does not necessarily take on the most obvious enemy, nor the one which causes the most anguish or concern, but chooses to engage where victory is certain. Breaking the hold of the weaker components of the spiritual foe will cause the greater forces to lose power, redistribute into weaker units, and become more vulnerable. As the weaker elements of the enemy forces fall, the stronger elements of those forces also become weak. They can eventually be attacked with ease and success.

The principle upon which this strategy works is that when a spiritual warrior is able to conquer one defect of character, that warrior gains power, confidence, and a connection to the Source that allows movement against other defects of character with greater force. In other words, if one can tackle some bad habits, one is more likely to be able to confront and defeat deeper character defects. As a snowball rolling downhill gains mass and momentum, the strength of the spiritual warrior grows as that warrior experiences victory in successive battles. Therefore, sometimes it is wiser to confront minor shortcomings first, such as unhealthy habits, gossiping, the tendency to dominate conversations, pessimism, and criticizing others, rather than to tackle more powerful enemies such as rage, greed, licentiousness, and conceit. These deeper defects must be dealt with at some point, but a spiritual warrior will find that experience in defeating minor defects helps when facing more formidable foes. This is the strategy of the orthodox method.

The unorthodox method is of a different nature, yet also quite effective. This method involves the element of surprise. That is, go where the enemy least expects you to go. If you are challenged time and again within the parameters of a particular earthly terrain, then choose another. If you find the enemy advancing within your thoughts on a particular subject, redefine it, refrain from it, replace it. Although everyone must have some routines in order to maintain a familiar and thus peaceful existence, to follow the same routine without variation is a prescription for disaster. You become vulnerable to the enemy and open for attack. Therefore, practice the unordinary. Change your routine. Walk a different path than the usual. Turn when you're least expected to turn. Pursue what you ordinarily would not pursue. Reach out where you would never reach. This keeps the enemy in suspense about where you will go next, and he is given no opportunity to study your weak points. As related in the *Tao Te Ching*, this is the way of the unorthodox:

> A good traveler has no fixed plans
> And is not intent upon arriving.
> A good artist lets his intuition
> Lead him wherever it wants.
> A good scientist has freed himself of concepts
> And keeps his mind open to what is.[1]

Believing in higher realities, in the battle of angels and demons over my soul, I see this unorthodox method as having real power over my spiritual enemies. If these demons are determined to attack me and destroy my spiritual health and well-being, how much simpler could I make it for them than to follow the same path every day? There is a saying that idleness is the devil's pillow, and how true this is, because when the warrior encamps in the same place and never moves, the enemy attacks often and at will. But if idleness is the devil's pillow, continuous routine is the devil's playground. Continuous routine gives the devils or demons all sorts of opportunities for mischief.

By changing my routine, I keep my personal demons off guard. If they would like to fill me with bouts of anxiety, the worst thing I could do is continue to enter with regular timing into arenas that bring about such anxiety. If something brings anxiety, then I do it differently, or not at all. Whatever I do, I make it unorthodox, and then the enemy becomes confused as to how to respond.

I have also found that when the enemy attacked me with bouts of depression, following the same old routine made it easy for it to keep watch on my every move. First, I realized that when I awakened in the mornings, I had a brief respite from depression, as if my demons were sleeping in a little longer than I was. But soon they would awaken and begin to fill me with melancholy thoughts and feelings, leading to despair by midday. Then I realized that if I could experience even that brief respite from demons in the morning, I didn't have to have them around at all. In fact, I was probably unconsciously inviting them into my life, most likely because I was following the same routine. When I changed my routine—like working at home for a day, taking a walk, not watching the usual programs on television, even sitting in a different place at supper, and changing bedtime and morning routines—the enemy couldn't keep up with me. The depression began to lift and to stay away. It was as if the enemy slept in only to awaken to find that I had moved camp in the meantime. The enemy waited in the usual places on the road of routine to ambush me, but I didn't show up anymore. Using the unorthodox method put me on a different path. Now, whether there really are demons looking to ambush us who can be outsmarted by a little unconventional warfare, or whether this process simply tricks our brains into secreting different chemicals giving us a different sensation of life, who cares? The fact is, this unorthodox method works.

Give yourself permission to practice the unorthodox. Follow the description of how to do this in the tasks at the end of this chapter. See what a difference it can make. Not only will it help you fight against your personal demons, it will also invigorate you, help your creativity, give you a lighter feeling, and introduce you to the vast and colorful variety of delightful experiences that life is ready to give you.

According to ancient Chinese masters, there are no more than five principal notes in a musical scale, yet in combination, they produce more sounds than could possibly be heard. There are only five principal colors, but their variations are so many that they cannot all be seen. There are only five principal flavors, but their variations are so many that they cannot all be tasted. For gaining strategic advantage in spiritual battle, there are only two principal approaches—namely the orthodox and the unorthodox—yet in combination, they produce inexhaustible possibilities. The orthodox and the unorthodox blend into each other like a circle with no beginning or end. Their possibilities are limitless.

When master warriors move against spiritual adversaries with the forces of the heavens behind them and the precision of the divine wisdom within them, no enemy can stand. When the speed of rushing water reaches the point where it can move boulders, this is the force of momentum. When the speed of a hawk is such that it can strike and kill, this is precision. So it is with skillful spiritual warriors—their force is swift and powerful, like a drawn catapult, and their precision is like releasing its trigger. Even in the middle of the tumult of spiritual battle, they cannot be confused. Even in the middle of the melee, with circumstances shifting all around them, they cannot be defeated. As Castaneda points out:

> A warrior is not a leaf
>   at the mercy of the wind.
> No one can push him;
> No one can make him do things
>   against himself
> Or against his better judgment.
> A warrior is tuned to survive,
> And he survives
>   in the best of all possible fashions.[2]

In spiritual battle, disorder in the enemy arises from order in oneself, cowardice arises in the enemy from courage in oneself, and weakness in the enemy arises from strength in oneself. To the degree that the warrior can master these, no destructive tendency can stand, and no spiritual enemy can gain a foothold. Whether demons or dysfunctions, they fall.

Order and disorder are a matter of organization in one's mind and actions; courage and cowardice are a matter of momentum in the heart of the spiritual warrior; strength and weakness are a matter of spiritual disposition. Therefore, those who are skillful at spiritual battle seek victory by organizing and dedicating themselves in such a way that they are able to gain momentum against their spiritual enemy, thus moving him into a position of vulnerability and then taking him with full force.

The expert in spiritual combat seeks victory from strategic advantage and does not act impulsively with crude force. The expert is able to select the appropriate actions against the spiritual aggressor in order to exploit the strategic advantage. The one who exploits the strategic advantage brings full spiritual forces into battle like rolling boulders down a steep hill. Boulders naturally rest on flat ground, but on steep ground, they roll. Therefore, when one strategically deploys inner forces against the spiritual adversary, it is like rolling boulders down a steep mountain. What can stand in their way?

❊ *Further Application*

Discovering Your Personal Priorities

It is organization that makes managing many challenges the same as managing a few. I recently received a call from a man named Bob. He had been attending our Spiritual Warfare Effectiveness Training program. Bob had a question which addresses this issue of organization and spiritual effectiveness.

He said to me, "I've been focusing on living with integrity and discovering my personal mission. I'm finding out that I do have some gifts that I can give to the world, and I've been a lot more active lately in helping people out and connecting with them. But my problem is that now I often find myself so busy that I feel like I'm neglecting my family. I promised to spend some extra time with the family for the holidays, but I look at my calendar and I've pretty well booked things up with work and volunteering to help some friends. I'm doing good things but I feel like I'm acting impulsively and am not in control. Truthfully, I'm feeling a bit guilty about the family. Any suggestions?"

"Do you prioritize responsibilities at work?" I asked. "Do you ever use a To Do list?"

"Why, of course," he responded. "I've got jobs coming in all the time, and things get so busy I wouldn't be able to function without the list, let alone prioritizing what needs to be done by when."

"Good. Now it's time to prioritize your values and come up with a To Do list for your personal life," I replied.

So often people are able to recognize the importance of prioritizing at the office, but neglect to consider what is important to them in their personal lives. In our conversation, Bob realized that his priorities were out of place because he never prioritized. Life just sort of happened to him, and he reacted accordingly and impulsively, only to pay for it later in time unspent at home, or in falling behind at work, and in the guilt he felt accordingly. In just a few moments of conscious thought Bob was able to list his general priorities. His family came first, then work, then extra activities such as volunteering to help others. He added that personal health came before everything or he wouldn't be able to take care of the other priorities. With that straight, Bob then promised to take some time to prioritize, on a piece of paper, the actions he desired to perform to meet these obligations. He promised to make a To Do list for his personal life, one which would include family at the top. He said, "I promised I'd do the bulk of the shopping this year for the holidays, and I'm not going to let that fall off the list. I can cut back on a few extracurricular activities, which will give me time with my son." He laughed. "Sometimes I feel like I'm obligated to do everything I see needs to be done, even if it's not my responsibility. There's an old saying, 'Take care of yourself first.' That can include my son, right?"

"Of course it can," I assured him. "In fact, if family isn't working, everything else has a tendency to fall apart. I think you're on the right track."

I saw Bob a few weeks later and asked him if he had made that To Do list.

"Did I make a list? I went through that first list in a week, and now I'm on number three! It's amazing when you write things down and pay attention how easily you're able to focus and get the jobs done that you should do and want to do. It seems so simple, as if I should have been doing this long ago. But I guess it's often the simple things we neglect."

I agree with Bob. Perhaps taking time to discover our personal priorities and forming a To Do list for our personal lives seems so simple that we neglect to do it. Yet it is such simple acts as these that keeps our lives uncomplicated and heading in the direction of our choosing. It is organization like this that makes managing what appears to be many challenges like managing a few.

Tasks

1. *Make a spiritual To Do list. List the changes you would like to make in your life, the issues left undone, and the challenges you know you need to face. Organize them according to their importance, with the most important as the number one priority for action and the rest following in order. When you are finished, examine the list. Is it accurate and realistic? Redefine items which call for a more accurate description and remove those which are not realistic. Determine how and when you will address the number one issue. Take action to address it. When you have made progress with this issue, move to the second, and so on. Update your list regularly, and be patient with yourself. You will never be able to clear the slate of issues. That is not the point. The point is to know the issues and to be able to take appropriate action leading to spiritual growth.*

2. *Experiment with the unorthodox. Change your routine, and notice the energy you receive from such changes. Have fun with this. For example, do your morning routine differently, take a different route to work, call someone you normally would not call and say hello. Try cooking some meals you wouldn't normally cook. Sleep in a different room for a night. Just for this day avoid a situation which brings spiritual challenges. Respond to a loved one's communication with an illogical response and then smile. Break the mold of your life and*

*keep the spiritual enemy guessing about
what you will do next. How does
it make you feel to do so?*

3. *Believe in and take advantage of spiritual
momentum. When things seem to be going
well, rejoice and continue in that joy. Do not
cut yourself short of joy. If you find movement
toward a better way of life, instead of stopping
for fear of too much change, take a few more
steps in the right direction. Believe in the
divine power which can work in you
and through you. Allow it to flow
freely with its incredible
healing force.*

Sun Tzu said:

    Those who are first on the battlefield and await the opponents are at ease; those who are last on the battlefield and head into battle get worn out. Therefore, good warriors cause others to come to them and do not go to others. What causes opponents to come of their own accord is the prospect of gain. What discourages opponents from coming is the prospect of harm. So when opponents are at ease, it is possible to tire them. When they are well fed, it is possible to starve them. When they are at rest, it is possible to move them. Appear where they cannot go; head for where they least expect you. To travel hundreds of miles without fatigue, go over land where there are no people. To unfailingly take what you attack, attack where there is no defense. For unfailingly secure defense, defend where there is no attack. So in the case of those who are skilled in attack, their opponents do not know where to defend. In the case of those skilled in defense, their opponents do not know where to attack.

CHAPTER 6

Emptiness and Fullness

*T*hose who first occupy the field of spiritual battle to await the enemy will be rested; those who wait for the spiritual battle without a plan will be ill-prepared when the enemy strikes and will soon become weary. Thus the expert in battle moves the enemy and is not moved by the enemy. Causing the spiritual enemy to attack of his own accord is a matter of making things easy for him; stopping the enemy from entering into your consciousness is a matter of obstructing him. Thus being able to wear down a well-rested enemy, to starve one that is well-provisioned, and to move one that is settled is a matter of taking actions which force the enemy to stay continually on the defensive. Appear where spiritual enemies cannot go, head for where they least expect you, and do what they would never consider you to do.

Unsettling a spiritual enemy who has set up camp within your being strikes at what he least expects you to attack. You can accomplish this aim by confronting a spiritual enemy you have never confronted before. Choose a destructive tendency which has been lulled to sleep by your acquiescence—one that would never expect to be attacked. The enemy may be so caught off guard that it easily surrenders or flees the field in a panic. Whatever it may be, if it is something you have never confronted before, such as idleness, or escapism, or procrastination, if you suddenly take it on with full force, this enemy is likely to flee in terror, without a fight. The master warrior can also starve a destructive tendency by not acting upon it. Desire,

75

without action, cannot survive, no matter what this desire might be. According to Swedenborg:

> Unless one does that which he desires
> There is within him a failure to desire,
> Which eventually becomes a lack of desire.[1]

If a destructive desire cannot find an outlet in action, it necessarily loses power over the warrior. By continual challenges, those spiritual enemies who do have a foothold in daily life are worn down and can eventually be defeated.

To travel hundreds of miles on your spiritual journey without fatigue, walk where there is no enemy presence. Survey your proposed destinations for danger; avoid questionable circumstances which may alert the enemy to your presence. Stop on your travels and listen and look, assessing the new terrain as you progress. Spiritual awareness can help you avoid a surprise ambush and needless battles. Cultivating full awareness of both the earthly terrain and its shifting patterns, and the changing spiritual climate accompanying you on your journey, will keep you prepared for any developing circumstances on either plane and allow you to choose your own battles rather than finding them thrust upon you. The average person wanders into predicaments which bring about temptation and anguish and is always on the defensive. The master warrior, however, looks ahead, sees what is coming and what may come in every new situation, and avoids spiritually dangerous circumstances. If the master warrior must walk through enemy territory, into situations which may bring about spiritual struggle and grief, that warrior walks softly, and silently, until the danger is passed. Therefore, Sun Tzu says:

> Become so veiled and subtle,
> That you have no form.
> Be so mysterious and miraculous,
> That you make no sound.

Thereby you become the director
Of your enemy's fate.

To attack without failure, attack what the enemy does not defend. To defend with the confidence of keeping one's well-being secure, defend what the enemy will not attack. So, in the case of the expert in attack, the enemy does not know where to defend; and in the case of the expert in defense, the enemy does not know where to strike. Observe what is being blessed in your life, and pursue it. If it is an action, do more of it. If it is a state of being, enjoy and value it. If it is a moment of good fortune, seize upon it. For to take full advantage of the good fortunes which befall you, whether in your spiritual campaign or on your earthly tour of duty, is to take ground which the enemy does not defend; and to surround oneself with the forces of what is good and spiritual, with all its blessings, is to defend what the enemy will not attack, because the powers against him are too great.

The art of spiritual warfare is a matter of emptiness and fullness. The expert at spiritual warfare empties the self of self—that is, of ego—and of all the wants, desires, misconceptions, and illusions which surround it. The expert replaces these aspects with a new self borne of the heavenly realm and of the Divine. This new self, being first empty and open to the inflow of what is good and blessed, is soon filled with what is good and blessed. Though it seems as if to empty oneself is to lose oneself, in reality, by so doing the spiritual warrior finds self. Though it seems as if the emptying out of self will result in the loss of inward life, in reality, the spiritual warrior finds life thereby. There is the appearance of death, but it is followed by the reality of life. Therefore, it is said:

Whoever desires to save his life
Will lose it,
And whoever loses his life for My sake,
Will find it.

(Matthew 16:25)

I know that I find myself facing a type of death every time I realize I need to let go of what I am holding onto. It feels like I am literally going to die, or something special that I care about will die, or some sense of control will die. If I stop worrying about my teenage children, will they not suddenly slide down the slippery slope into juvenile delinquency? If I let go of obsessing about what that person thinks of me, won't that person immediately dislike me? If I don't control every aspect of my work and push harder and harder, will I not be fired tomorrow? These are questions my mind asks when I am forced to confront the reality that I must let go. In letting go of the fear, the codependency, the need to control, I can feel as if I will lose everything. And, indeed, a death does take place. Another part of that worrisome, controlling, obsessive, fearful, destructive me dies. The emptiness is almost unbearable. But it is soon filled with wholeness. It is soon filled with freedom, trust, self-esteem, serenity. Losing one kind of life, I gain another. The appearance is death, but through such death comes real life.

To advance against a spiritual enemy without resistance, burst through the enemy's weak points; to withdraw elusively, outguess him. Therefore, if you want to do battle, the enemy has no choice, even though he lies safe behind the high walls and deep moats of the inner recesses of your mind, because you strike at what he must rescue. If you do not want to fight, the enemy cannot engage you, even though you have no more than a line drawn in the sand to protect you, because you set him off on the wrong track. If you can make the enemy show his position while concealing your own from him, you will be at full force where he is divided. The only way to achieve this goal is by making quick decisions to move in another direction, either in anticipation of an enemy approach, or even before such anticipation. If you keep moving, changing, reshaping your strategy, you keep him off balance. Therefore, when you induce your spiritual opponent to construct a formation while you yourself are formless, then you are concentrated while your opponent is fragmented. When you are centered into a oneness of thought and intention, and your enemy is divided a thousandfold out of confusion, then the odds of victory in an attack are in your favor.

If you can strike few spiritual foes with much force, you will thus minimize the number of those with whom you do battle. The master of spiritual combat chooses to challenge only one spiritual enemy at a time. If harassed by a multitude of inner enemies, for instance, creating such things as impatience, anger, desire, and loathing, the master of spiritual combat does not confront all of these traits at the same time. Not even the most skilled warrior could win such a battle. But to tackle the weakest of the multitude is wisdom, for the warrior's focus remains precise, and the full force against the single enemy remains intact. Perhaps the warrior takes on impatience first, vanquishes that foe, and then turns to challenge anger with new strength and resolve. As one enemy falls the others are weakened. As victory is achieved over the one, others can then be taken.

Sun Tzu says that the place and time you have chosen to give the enemy battle must be a surprise to him. If he cannot anticipate you, the positions the enemy must prepare to defend will be many, and any particular point you engage in battle will have fewer in number. Therefore, if the enemy makes preparations by reinforcing his numbers at the front, his rear is weakened; if he makes preparations at the rear, his front is weakened; if he makes them on his left flank, his right is weakened; if he makes them on his right flank, his left is weakened. When you force the enemy to be prepared everywhere, he becomes everywhere weakened. Therefore, to attack one spiritual enemy, do battle until some ground is gained, and then retreat for awhile before taking on another. To continue to fight constantly against one inward foe, at the neglect of the others, allows the enemy to reinforce that foe endlessly. For instance, the one who is concerned with only a single spiritual flaw for the duration of life remains a prisoner of all the rest throughout life. It is a useless battle and a waste of military resources and might. The spiritual warrior then tires and loses the heart to fight at all. But to rest from one foe only to attack another—to make progress and then to rest before attacking still another—is a way of keeping the enemy guessing where the next battlefield will be. It also gives the spiritual warrior an opportunity to take ground in different areas of life, and thus to grow.

One is weak who is forced to make preparations against others, but one who makes others prepare against him has strength. So, if you can anticipate when and where a spiritual battle will take place, you can march into battle prepared and well-rested. But if you cannot anticipate when and where such battle will take place, your ability to defend yourself will be limited, and you will quickly lose heart. How much more so when you have lost connection with the Source, because your consciousness is fragmented on the field of spiritual battle? Therefore, remain alert as you traverse new terrain and be able to anticipate when a battle may stir within you. If you are aware, you will know when, for example, feelings of inadequacy will try to bring you down. Circumstances which cause such bouts with feelings of inadequacy and self-doubt cannot be avoided, but if you are aware when such bouts are likely to occur, you can go into battle prepared rather than caught off guard, with strength and resolve rather than with weakness. This is true for each and every spiritual enemy you may confront. To be awake and aware, and thus prepared for battle, turns the ordinary person into the master warrior in spiritual growth. The Buddha observed:

> Wakefulness is the way of life.
> The fool sleeps
> As if he were already dead,
> But the master is awake
> And he lives forever.[2]

To sum up: The number of forces against you makes no difference with respect to victory; for it is said that victory can be created. Even though the enemy has the strength in numbers, you can prevent him from using his full force. As the warriors of old have said, if one relies on the Divine, one need not fear the number of the enemy:

> The Lord is my light and my salvation;
> Whom shall I fear?
> The Lord is the strength of my life;
> Of whom shall I be afraid?
> When the wicked came against me to eat up my flesh,
> My enemies and my foes,
> They stumbled and fell.
> Though an army should encamp against me,
> My heart shall not fear;
> Though war should rise against me,
> In this I will be confident.
>
> (Psalm 27:1-3)

Therefore, analyze the enemy's battle array to understand its strengths and weaknesses; provoke him to find out the pattern of his movements; induce him to adopt specific means of action; skirmish with him to find out where he is strong and where weak.

The ultimate skill in taking up a strategic position is to have no form. If your position is formless, the most intelligent and crafty enemy spies will not be able to find out anything to use against you. The enemy cannot form a strategy. Avoid uniformity and the conventional. Avoid routine, for it puts the mind, and thus the soul, to sleep. Practice creativity and explore the unconventional, for this action enlivens the warrior spirit. Be unpredictable and the spiritual enemy will not be able to predict your destination or spiritual maneuvers. Victory over multitudes of the dark forces is a matter of positioning oneself against them. However, though the victories may appear the same, the positioning always changes. Therefore, victory in spiritual warfare is not repetitive but adapts its form endlessly.

Creating strategic military formation against the inner foe is like water. Just as the flow of water avoids high ground and rushes to the lowest point, so on the path to victory avoid the enemy's strong points and strike where he is weak. As water varies its flow according to the fall of the land, so vary your methods of gaining victory according to the enemy's disposition. Military force in spiritual combat has no constant formation, just as water has no constant shape; the ability to gain victory by changing and adapting according to the opponent is the mark of spiritual genius.

❋ Further Application
Pursuing What You Love

One way to experience growth is to observe what is being blessed in your life, and pursue it. If it is an action, do more of it. If it is a state of being, enjoy and value it. If it is a moment of good fortune, seize upon it.

Often a person will say he or she loves to do something but doesn't have the time to do it more often. Or how often have you heard someone say, "I wish I could do that," and you know full well that they can, but they don't. One of the promises I've made myself is that when I'm on my deathbed (hopefully not too soon), I'm not going to reflect on my life and mutter, "If only I had . . . if only I had played more. If only I had shown more gratitude and love. If only I had written that book. If only I had spent more time with the family." What a nightmare—to have had the ability, opportunity, desire, but not to have acted! The real joy of pursuing what you love and what is bringing blessing into your life is that the blessing grows. Jesus said, "Give and it will be given unto you: good measure, pressed down, shaken together, and running over will be put into your bosom. For with the same measure that you use, it will be measured back to you again" (Luke 6:38). To the degree that we capitalize on the gifts and blessings God has given us, sending them out into the world, we receive as much, and often more in return. When we act on what we love, especially if it is of useful service to others, our hearts are filled with joy—abundant, overflowing, revitalizing, uplifting—giving meaning to our beings. To live this way is to follow our blessings.

I know I've gone through times of doubt when good fortune arrives. I've said to myself, "I'm not worthy," and failed to enjoy the good fortune. When doors have opened for new avenues of blessing and growth, I've felt twinges of fear and inadequacy and have stood paralyzed waiting for the doors of opportunity to close before my eyes. What I realized was that the only thing holding me back from going through those doors or enjoying myself when fortune smiled upon me were spiritual enemies. Fear, doubt, inertia, even self-loathing would stop me from going through those doors. It wasn't until I recognized that these enemies were holding me back from being a more useful, productive, and happy person that I began to march through those doors of opportunity. I would not let them hold me down. And it is surprising how quickly those enemies disappeared as I allowed the real blessings of God to enter my life and my consciousness. Some of my means have been getting involved in more counseling, which I love, as well as in men's work and in writing books. I have sought the courage to stand in the public forum in front of hundreds and be myself. When I take the risk, the reward always comes back to me in the way of more blessings. The joy I have felt from not limiting my life, or selling myself short of pursuing the dreams my Creator has put before me, has been nothing but a blessing. Find what God is blessing in your life and do more of it. You won't be disappointed with the results.

Tasks

1. *If you are being challenged by a spiritual enemy—some destructive tendency or defect of character which continues to attack you—ask yourself what it is about the earthly terrain you are walking which allows that enemy to gain strategic advantage. Change your earthly terrain—the circumstances which enable that enemy—and watch the battle turn in your favor.*

2. *Practice foresight. Look at some areas in your spiritual life which are creating a challenge or giving you concern. If nothing changes in your opinions, actions, or circumstances, where will you be with these challenges in one year from now? How about in two years? What effect will they have on your life? What action do you need to take now to alter the future for the better?*

3. *Have you been working on the same character defect for too long? Is it time to retreat from that particular battlefront for awhile and approach another enemy? If so, do so. What benefits do you gain?*

Sun Tzu Said:

Nothing is harder than armed struggle. The difficulty of armed struggle is to make long distances near and make problems into advantages. . . . Therefore, armed struggle is considered profitable, and armed struggle is considered dangerous. . . . So a military force is established by deception, mobilized by gain, and adapted by division and combination.

Therefore, when it moves swiftly it is like the wind, when it goes slowly it is like the forest; it is rapacious as fire, immovable as mountains. It is as hard to know as the dark; its movement is like pealing thunder. . . .

Surviving
Spiritual
Struggle

There is nothing more difficult than armed struggle against a spiritual opponent, for the enemy works against the spiritual warrior through the warrior's own thoughts, feelings, and impulses. Spiritual combat is waged over what one chooses to value in life and what one chooses to love above all things. The inner clash of weapons and armor, which brings such torturous pain and exhausting struggle, is the confrontation between what is evil and good, what is false and true, and what is life-giving and life-threatening within the warrior's own mind and heart. This combat is waged by opposing forces in the spiritual realm who fight over the individual's life and soul. Yet the battle is not removed from the spiritual warrior's consciousness. On the contrary, it is intensely perceived. Every collision of spiritual forces, every skirmish, every individual parry and returning blow of every soldier on this inner battlefield, is embodied in the warrior's memories, judgments, and choices. Therefore, the pain of the inner battle is real and acute.

In the heat of the battle the spiritual warrior can feel ripped apart by conflicting desires. The battle becomes a struggle of the self with the self, both selves determined to survive and bent on destroying the other. The struggle can become exhausting, seemingly to the point of death, but it is a battle worth waging.

> If one man conquer in battle
> A thousand men,

And if another conquer himself,
He is the greatest of conquerors.[1]

In the smoke and confusion of battle, the warrior can also become disoriented. That which is good can appear evil, and that which is evil can appear good. That which is false can appear true, and that which is true can appear false. As the spiritual battle intensifies, the warrior can even become uncertain about the nature of the enemy himself. The danger of joining the ranks of one's enemy, and attacking one's own troops in the confusion, is a very real possibility. Dazed by the din of battle, the master warrior must hold fast to the day's strategy and muster the courage to persevere.

What is difficult in armed struggle is to turn the long and torturous into the direct route and to turn adversity into advantage. But the advantages are great and many, because through victory in such inward conflict the warrior gains spiritual ground and new freedom. Through victory in spiritual conflict the warrior becomes strong, wise, and truly spiritual. Thus, armed struggle can be profitable, but it can also be dangerous.

Therefore, in the heat of spiritual battle, the warrior must rely on maneuvers which are deceptive to the enemy but familiar to oneself. To establish your ground, calculate advantages in deciding your movements and consolidate your forces to make your strategic changes. In the heat and confusion of battle, especially if you are being thrust backward by the enemy, you may abandon any particular course of action on the field, but do not abandon your overall strategy. In spiritual warfare, the warrior's sense of reality can shift with the shifting tides of the battle. One can feel outnumbered even while overpowering the enemy. Victory can appear lost when it is about to be gained. Some spiritual warriors give up the battle just as it is turning toward victory, because of fear, confusion, lack of will, and cowardice. This is tantamount to throwing away victory and embracing defeat. Know, therefore, that when the smoke of the battle brings confusion, illusions abound.

Rather than basing your strategic movements upon the smoke and shadows of war and the uncertainty of will which follows, rely on common sense and what you considered to be true before entering the fray. After the smoke begins to clear and the dust settles, you can then reassess without risk of catastrophic errors in military judgment. This is the way of surviving armed struggle in its most tumultuous hour.

It is easy to make clear decisions about the direction of your life when it seems to be going fairly well and you aren't dealing with any particular challenges. It is quite another thing when you are thrown into the midst of temptation and spiritual battle. Then the confusion begins, and with it, the inclination to abandon previous aspirations only to grasp recklessly at what looks like a quick solution or a compromise that doesn't seem as difficult. This way of proceeding usually leads to disaster.

Therefore, in the heat and smoke of battle, when alternate choices arise, stick to the original plan until the battle is over. If the new choice seems right, then consider it with care, but if it disappears as the desire disappears, with the smoke and confusion, know that you have escaped defeat.

> The end of desire is the end of sorrow
> The fool is his own enemy.[2]

An ancient book of military discipline says that in the heat of conflict, "Words are not heard, so cymbals and drums are made. Owing to lack of visibility, banners and flags are made." Such devices were used by armies of old to focus and unify soldiers' ears and eyes. Once people were unified, the brave did not have to advance alone, nor were the cowardly permitted to retreat alone. This is an allegory, containing lessons for the spiritual warrior as well. Even as cymbals, drums, banners, and flags were used to focus and unify armies, the spiritual warrior relies upon spiritual markers and means of communication. The wisdom sayings, religious teachings, mandates, and spiritual instruction of the world's great traditions can be such guides in the midst of conflict. Like a mantra, repeat them in your mind over and over again to maintain your focus and to stay unified in your purpose.

In my Spiritual Warfare Effectiveness Training course, we gather wisdom teaching from various religious writings, warrior-philosophers, and sages and memorize those we think might serve us well in battle. One man has said that the one he uses every day to distinguish between what is his and what is thrust upon him by his obsessive, compulsive nature is the saying of Sun Tzu quoted previously:

> If you know the enemy and yourself
> You will never be at risk in a hundred battles;
> If you do not know the enemy but know yourself
> You will sometimes win and sometimes lose;
> If you know neither the enemy nor yourself
> You will be at risk in every battle.

Another "marker" we learn in our spiritual warrior training is something we encourage the warrior to verbalize every morning upon awakening:

> Today I will act without expectation;
> I will fight without aggression;
> I will call upon a higher power for my aid;
> I will confront the forces of darkness in my life,
> And I will claim the victory.[3]

I have the above quotation pasted to my wall just above my dresser. I can't help but see it in the morning and use it. It reminds me of what is important in my life and of what I want to do and stand for that day. Another one that I use often, especially when I enter the battlefield with fear and anxiety, is the Twenty-third Psalm:

> The Lord is my Shepherd; I shall not want.
> He makes me to lie down in green pastures;

He leads me beside the still waters.
He restores my soul;
He leads me in the paths of righteousness
For His name's sake.
Yea, though I walk through the valley
 of the shadow of death,
I will fear no evil; for You are with me;
Your rod and Your staff, they comfort me.
You prepare a table before me in the
 presence of my enemies;
You anoint my head with oil; my cup runs over.
Surely goodness and mercy shall follow me
All the days of my life;
And I will dwell in the house of the Lord
Forever.

These sayings are especially useful as markers in times of heavy battle, for they keep the warrior focused in the right direction. Likewise, gather your own markers and become so familiar with them that you can remember them in spiritual battle.

Maintain connection to the Source at all times. Keep lines of communication open and supplies flowing to the center of the conflict. When communication with the Source is cut off, oversight is lost, directions confused, and maneuvering haphazard. Loss of supplies means loss of power and sustenance. Defeat is inevitable. Therefore, in brutal conflict, though attention is focused upon each move of the enemy, your position relative to the Source must be known at all times, and communication must remain open. If communication is lost, or supplies depleted, retreat and regroup. To move against a spiritual foe without sufficient supplies and communication is an act not of bravery but of folly. To die alone on the spiritual battlefield, when one might have lived in victory, is the mark not of a hero, but of a fool. Therefore, stay close to the Source, especially in times of great need and adversity.

Hear my cry, O God;
Attend to my prayer.
From the end of the earth
I will cry to you,
When my heart is overwhelmed . . .
For you have been a shelter for me,
And a strong tower from the enemy.
I will dwell in your tent forever;
I will trust in the shelter of your wings.

(Psalm 61:1-4)

When entering unfamiliar terrain, use local guides. Those who have walked the path you are now taking have much to offer in the way of knowledge and support. When relying on local guides, choose those who have done battle on these same fields and have gained victory. These people can offer not only knowledge, but wisdom. They can help you to see what you may not see on your own. They can give you foresight and the upper hand against the enemy. They can support you where you need support the most, both in direction and morale.

I have enjoyed the company of many good companions along the way through various types of spiritual growth and support groups. The one I find most helpful is a men's support group that has been together for nearly five years. I know these men intimately, and we have shared our victories and defeats, our dreams and our fears, our strengths and our shortcomings. They watch my back, and I watch theirs. They lend support and show me the way when I cannot support myself or see clearly. They listen and are there for me. My battles are easier because of them, and victory is more certain.

It is important to find good companions on your spiritual journey who can support you. Think of what useful and pleasant outcomes can be achieved from having a good business partner, for instance. Those who have had bad partners learn the hard way how important character becomes. Without basics such as integrity and mutual trust, the day-to-day handling of all business affairs can not only be unpleasant to deal with, but end up being a disaster. On the other hand, coming into a partnership with one who has traveled a similar path, who is trustworthy and walks not only with integrity but with a true regard for friendship, will no doubt be a blessing and maximize potential for the whole endeavor. This is no different in life's partnerships. Find those on a similar path, with similar goals, who are willing to both receive and offer support. Those who have much in common with you have probably battled the same demons and know the battlefields you share quite well. They can be of great help to you, and vice versa. As stated in a Chinese military classic:

> If you suffer the same illness as other people,
> And you all aid each other;
> If you have the same emotions and complete each other;
> The same hatreds and assist each other;
> And the same likes and seek them together—
> Then without any armored soldiers
> You will win.[4]

Sun Tzu says it is very possible that an entire enemy army can be demoralized and that its commander can be made to lose heart. In the morning of war, the enemy's morale is high; by noon, it begins to decline; by evening, it drains away. Thus the expert in spiritual warfare avoids the enemy when his morale is high and strikes when the enemy's morale is low. Elude the enemy in his time of morning. Do not march on fields where you can be seen. Attack him in his evening, when he cannot muster the force to defeat you.

Using order to deal with the disorderly, practicing calm to deal with the clamorous, is equivalent to mastering the heart. Standing your ground while waiting for the distant enemy to come near, meeting the weary enemy in comfort, confronting the hungry enemy with a full stomach, involves mastering strength. Avoiding confrontation with overpowering enemy forces is to master adaptation. The rule for military operations is not to face an uphill fight and not to oppose those who hold a position on higher ground.

Do not follow a feigned retreat.

Do not attack crack troops.

Do not swallow the enemy's bait.

Do not obstruct an enemy returning home; in surrounding the enemy, leave him a way out; do not press an enemy that is cornered. This is the art of surviving armed struggle.

The one who understands the tactic of converting the torturous into the direct route will take the victory. Never lose sight of the final goal, even in times of frustration and pain. There will be occasions in battle when the warrior feels that all is lost. Do not lose heart. This is the turning point in the battle. The end is near. Victory is within grasp.

This, then, is the end of spiritual conflict. The spirit borne of battle becomes mature and refined. It grows in wisdom, yet captures and maintains youthful zeal. When it moves swiftly it is like the wind; when it proceeds slowly and majestically, it is like the forest. The spirit is as fierce as fire against inward foes, yet as immovable as a mountain. It is as unpredictable as a shadow; its action is like lightning and thunder.

❋ Further Application

Stick With Your Strategy

One scenario in which I found myself changing strategy was in my efforts to quit smoking over the years. My peacetime plan was to quit cold turkey and never smoke again. Sometimes I would make it for a few years. But then I would find myself on a men's weekend where everyone was lighting up cigars, or after a good meal with a smoker friend of mine who was lighting up, and suddenly the temptation would come upon me.

Instead of relying on the clear perception I once had that any contact with nicotine would be a disaster, I would switch plans within seconds. The new plan I'd adopt as I impulsively lit up was based on the false premise that I can smoke a cigar occasionally without getting hooked. I'd tell myself that I could smoke just this once, or maybe even once a month. Cigars or pipes, I'd reason, are not the same as cigarettes. But with the cigar in my mouth, I became addicted immediately. The same thing happens to alcoholics. It is easy to see clearly the consequences of one drink when in a time of inner peace and healthy sobriety. But when the battle rages and the potential for a drink is truly at hand, so many deceptions arise, and one can make the mistake of taking that drink, truly believing that this alternate plan of battle is not surrender. In these and other conflicts, when things look complicated and you start considering alternative plans, remember that it is only as complicated as you make it and stick to the strategy you had before the battle began.

This principle also holds true in relationships. I think every married person has experienced the dilemma at one time or another of the marriage being challenged by the potential for infidelity, real or imagined. I have become especially aware of this struggle through intimate conversations with those who have confided their inclination toward sexual or relationship addiction. I believe more and more people are realizing that sex and romantic love can be as addictive as any drug. Anyone who is keenly aware of that dark void in his or her heart, which cannot seem to be filled, will turn to whatever brings a sense of wholeness and relief, no matter how fleeting or damaging in the long run. That is, they will until they begin to deal with it on a spiritual level and allow that void to be filled with the healing of a Higher Power. But this can only be attained through persevering in spiritual battle.

One man described to me how much he loved his wife, believed in their marriage, and would want nothing to hurt his three children. But that was when there were no women around paying him special attention. During his fifteen years of marriage, he had gone through a series of friendships with single women. These liaisons became more and more intimate and affectionate until they threatened to destroy his marriage, not to mention the potential damage to himself and the other woman. After one such relationship actually did almost break up his marriage, in his struggle to put his life back into order he found a group of people who dealt with romantic love and sexual addiction, and he started a new life. Upon reflecting on how he used to fight against his own selfish wants, lusts, and misguided longing for love, he realized that part of his problem in these relationships was that he'd switch plans in the middle of his spiritual battle. In one conversation, he explained it to me this way:

"I would meet this girl at work, and there would be an instant attraction. At that point I'd be pretty clear that I didn't want to get involved in something heavy again that would hurt my marriage. But then because of my addictive nature, I guess, it wouldn't stop there. We'd start having long conversations, a lot of laughs. Then it would lead to coffee in the cafeteria at break times. And then it would go on to rendezvous after work. I was an expert at being the nice male listener, the one who could show compassion and unconditional love. This usually led to the woman falling in love with me. At that point, I felt high on the love and attention I was getting, but didn't want it to go any further. In fact, I realized that what I truly didn't want to happen was happening again. Sometimes it would go even farther, but then, thank God, either I would get my act together and begin to pull out of the relationship, or the other woman would eventually fall out of love and leave me.

"But here's the thing. I had rules for myself, but in the heat of the temptation I'd flounder and change them. One rule was that it was OK to have friendships with the opposite sex but not to talk about things I wouldn't talk about in front of my wife. Another rule was not to meet with women outside the office or for some quasi-date. Another rule was to share with my wife what was happening if some issue came up. Another rule I had was to remember how much I do love my wife and wouldn't want to betray her in any way. How did it all go wrong? In the middle of the battle my emotions played in, and the lies started flooding through the gates:

What would one innocent cup of coffee across the street hurt?

This woman needs me. I can't shut her down by keeping our conversation off intimate subjects.

As long as I don't have sex with her, I can have a healthy friendship with her and with my wife.

My wife wouldn't understand our friendship, so I don't think I'll tell her about it.

The more sensible part of me would be screaming, "This isn't the plan! You're changing the rules! It didn't work before. It's not going to work now!" But in all of that confusion, I'd begin to change the plan. It wouldn't be as obvious as, 'OK, change in plan, have sex with her.' It would be more subtle, innocent, just a shift in perspective, a small alteration of my course, but inevitably these small changes added up to abandoning much of what I really wanted, or at least what the noble part of me really wanted out of life. I've learned a lot since then. I've learned that maybe I can't handle what some others can in this arena. I pay attention to the triggers that get me going. I try to be honest with myself about my dark side, and I talk about it with people who understand me. I have also learned that allurement is a natural part of life and that inner struggles will come with all kinds of illusions. In those times, it's suicide to change the plan. Stick to the plan, and the struggle will pass."

Tasks

1. *Every spiritual warrior needs a time of rest and recreation. No one can survive spiritual warfare if continually in battle. Plan a special time to abandon your routine and recreate. If you cannot find the courage to do this, you are a prisoner to a powerful spiritual enemy. You must take action. Plan a day from work for rest, recreation, rejuvenation. If you are able, make it a weekend away from home just for you. Treat yourself to something physically and emotionally rewarding: a massage, a dinner out, a movie, a few hours alone with a good book, or something else just for you. See what difference it makes with your outlook on the battle.*

2. *If you are in the middle of a spiritual battle and, because of the smoke and din of war, are now confused about what is true and what decisions or actions would be most spiritually beneficial, stop and reflect. Ask yourself what you believed would be a good and right decision before the battle commenced. Follow that prior course until the smoke clears. Then reassess.*

3. *Do you have a confidant with whom to share some of your struggles? Everyone needs at least one. Look for someone safe, grounded, and growing. Make friends. If your spiritual enemies are addictions or compulsions for which there are support groups, join one. You need allies in spiritual warfare.*

Sun Tzu said:

Let there be no encampment on difficult terrain. Let diplomatic relations be established at borders. Do not stay in barren or isolated territory. When on surrounded ground, plot. When on deadly ground, fight. There are routes not to be followed, armies not to be attacked, citadels not to be besieged, territory not to be fought over, orders of civilian governments not to be obeyed.

Therefore, the considerations of the intelligent always include both benefit and harm. As they consider benefit, their work can expand; as they consider harm, their troubles can be resolved. . . .

Therefore, there are five traits that are dangerous in generals. Those who are ready to die can be killed; those who are intent on living can be captured; those who are quick to anger can be shamed; those who are puritanical can be disgraced; those who love people can be troubled. These five things are faults in generals and disasters for military operations.

Adaptations

Only one who is flexible and able to adapt to varying circumstances, terrain, and enemy maneuvers will gain victory. Think about this in marriage and love relationships. People who marry believing that they will live happily ever after without going through what amounts to a process of continual change are dreaming. Marriage is about adapting and growing. Love is about the willingness to be flexible. The same is true in business: when one loses the ability to adapt to current trends, one can lose the war of competition. As other companies were responding to the public's hunger for variety, Ford refused to adapt, pontificating that the public could have any color car they wanted, as long as it was black. That inflexibility cost the Ford company millions of dollars and the loss of the upper hand for years. How much more does this inflexibility hurt one's spiritual prospects? One must prepare one's self to be flexible in all circumstances. Preparation provides the way for flexibility; flexibility provides the way for adaptation; and adaptation provides the way for victory.

While preparing for spiritual warfare, form alliances with those who intersect your path and share common interests and objectives, for these can become companions in spiritual battle and confidants for life. Seek allies in the spiritual realm as well, with heavenly forces who offer their camaraderie and support, for these will fight by your side even under the most savage enemy assault, until victory is achieved. As the remarkably accomplished warrior Helen Keller has written:

When I review my life,
It seems to me
That my most precious obligations
Are to those whom I have never seen.
My dearest intimacies
Are those of my mind;
My most loyal and helpful friends
Are those of the spirit.[1]

In preparing for spiritual combat, do not encamp on difficult terrain. It is hard enough to hold one's position on favorable ground when attacked by the forces of destruction. When you find yourself on ground surrounded by the spiritual enemy, plot. When you realize you have entered deadly ground, fight. There are pathways not to be traveled, spiritual armies not to be attacked, well protected enemies not to be assaulted, territory not to be contested, and even rules not to be obeyed.

Therefore, master warriors who know how to adapt and take advantage of the various grounds of battle know how to win in spiritual warfare. The spiritual warriors who do not know how to adapt, even if they occupy familiar territory, do not know how to take advantage of it. Even if they are very powerful and know what can be gained through spiritual victory, they cannot achieve it.

For this reason, the wise warrior always considers the benefit as well as the harm of each strategic maneuver. Concentrating on the benefits, the wise warrior is able to maximize usefulness and service to self and others. Concentrating on the potential harm, the wise warrior is able to avoid what is hurtful and to resolve difficulties.

When a person faces a tough decision, it is all too common to spend a great deal of emotional energy worrying about what to do rather than using some good old fashion military discipline to help with the decision. Whether the decision is about family, career, relationships, business transactions, or deeper issues of spiritual life, sometimes sitting down with a piece of paper, or in front of the computer, and summing up the benefit and the harm of each decision can give a person the added insight in making the right choices. A military strategist knows that this work must be done in order to maximize the opportunity for victory and minimize the potential for catastrophe. The same thing can hold true for the important decisions of our lives.

What are some questions which this benefit/harm analysis might be useful in answering? Certainly, those regarding any major life decisions. Should I take this job? Should I marry this person? Is it time for children? Should we move? Is divorce the right decision? Should I make the sacrifice? Would it be wise to confront him? Should I tell? Would it be best to go forward with this agreement or back out? Should I take care of myself this time or bow to his needs again? Can I afford to do so much? Would more time help? Is this the right thing to do? Taking the time to analyze the benefit and the harm of any decision will only help bring clarity and right action.

To be adaptable means to be open and willing to redefine every circumstance, to rethink every strategy, and to be able to change course if necessary. To be prepared for spiritual warfare does not mean to be certain, for certainty in spiritual battle, more often than not, becomes blind assumption. The master warrior never rides into battle on the conviction of absolute truth, for truth is infinite and in itself unfathomable, and even the wisest warrior, at best, is finite and limited in comprehension. It is better to ride on faith. To have faith in battle is to believe humbly, for the mind then stays open to all possibilities. The desire remains intact to act upon those possibilities. On the other hand, to go into the battle with certainty that one knows the truth is to ride blind into the fray. One who says "I know" knows nothing compared to the one who says "I believe."

There have been many spiritual warriors throughout the ages, who, in the name of their God, and with utter assurance of the truth, have used this assurance as a justification to persecute those who believe differently. How many people, in the name of their God, have condemned others of different convictions? How many have looked upon those of a different faith as of lesser value and a lower class of humanity? How many, in the assurance of their convictions, have feared others with differing opinions and even placed upon them the label of evil, violently assaulting them in the name of righteousness? The answer is, too many. Absolute truth no doubt exists, but the certainty that one holds this perfect knowledge comes not from God, but from spiritual arrogance, intolerance, fear, and hatred of others. This belief is enemy propaganda, spread among the armies of spirit to turn them against each other.

The master warrior learns to adapt, not only in preparation for—or even during—battle, but also in the event of defeat. It is especially in times of defeat that the spiritual warrior must not lose heart, but cling to hope, for hope is real. Once the enemy has defeated the warrior on a particular battlefield, the propaganda of falsehood begins. The spiritual enemy employs every means to convince the warrior that all is hopeless. Through all manner of lies and twisted stories, the enemy endeavors to persuade the spiritual warrior that the war is over and that spiritual defeat is permanent. But let it be known that as long as the spiritual warrior walks on earthly terrain the light of hope shines on that path and illumines the way to victory. No defeat is permanent, for the Divine provides that each warrior may be lifted out of defeat to new ground. If the warrior is willing—for it is a matter of choice—each day provides a new beginning, fresh supplies, forces, and opportunity for victory. This is the way to victory, even in the throes of defeat:

> When you begin a great work
> You can't expect to finish it all at once;
> Therefore . . . press on,
> And let nothing discourage you
> Till you have entirely finished what you have begun. . . .
>
> As for me, I assure you I will press on,

And the contrary winds may blow strong in my face
Yet I will go forward and never turn back,
And continue to press forward
Until I have finished.[2]

Therefore, be flexible in all situations. When in battle, prepare for victory; when in defeat, prepare for battle. The rule of military operations is not to count on opponents not coming, but to be prepared to deal with them; not to rely on opponents not attacking, but to rely on having what cannot be attacked; not to enter into spiritual serfdom when defeated, but to begin the rebellion anew.

There are five faults in spiritual warriors: Those who are ready to die spiritually can be killed spiritually because they have an inward desire to become one with the darkness; those who are intent on eluding the pain of inward struggle can be captured, for they are not willing to fight; those who are overcome with guilt and grief upon losing a battle will remain prisoner, for they can be shamed into acquiescence; those who are puritanical will be disgraced, for they can be blindsided by the enemy; those who desire to please others at the expense of self can be troubled, for they do not fight their own battles.

These five faults in spiritual warriors are potentially disastrous in spiritual warfare. When approaching any spiritual combat, search the interiors of your being to find the modus operandi of your heart. One's intentions can be changed and purposes revised, but one can never completely reverse the devastation of an ill-fated battle. Therefore, when assessing the circumstances of war, take the long view from higher ground, and judge wisely. In the classic guide to strategy, A *Book of Five Rings*, Miyamoto Musashi advises us:

With your spirit open and unconstricted,
Look at things from a higher point of view.[3]

❈ Further Application

Considering the Benefit and the Harm

Virtually everyone has heard the story of the codependent spouse who finds him/herself trapped in a relationship with a partner whose alcohol or drug addiction is destroying their lives, but who cannot come to make the decision to take appropriate action which could lead to healing. But it may seem ludicrous to someone who has not experienced this disease to hear that it truly debilitates one's ability to reason, and to act, especially on behalf of one's self. Any discipline or process of analysis will help in this regard. I recently heard first-hand the story of a recovering codependent who used this benefit/harm analysis to help guide her in the right direction in confronting her spouse. She told a fairly typical story of watching her husband slowly lose control of his drinking, the growing emotional distance, the abusive language to her and her children, the promises broken, the money disappearing, the lies, the excuses. She had nagged and cajoled him, but was too afraid to confront him with an ultimatum. She knew it was the only viable choice left to save herself and her family and to give him an opportunity to get on the road to recovery. However, the thought of an ultimatum frightened her. She said she truly loved him and, curiously enough, didn't want to hurt him by threatening to leave. Also, she feared that if he didn't respond, her children might not go along with her, and where would she go anyway? She had often felt that perhaps living in this situation was better than living alone, or hurting the children through what could end up being a "messy divorce."

However, she did see a counselor once, who suggested that she sit down and write out the benefits and the harm of two decisions. What would be the benefit and the harm of doing nothing? What would be the benefit and the harm of laying down the ultimatum and having to go through her threats, if she must? She found that when she added up the potential harm of doing nothing, her mind was already made up. When she looked at the potential benefits of having her husband respond to this type of intervention, she realized the risk was worth it. She also realized that even in the worst scenario she wouldn't be living a lie anymore and that, whether she liked it or not, she felt confrontation at this stage was "the right thing."

Before confronting him she spoke to her children, her husband's immediate relatives, and two friends she felt she could trust. Her children were present for the confrontation. As she spoke to her husband, she did so from love and yet from a firmness she had not experienced within herself before. His first reaction was one of disbelief, then sadness. Then he said, "I'll think about it and give you an answer tomorrow." She agreed. Then next day he said, "I've got a trip to Atlanta I have to take on Saturday, but I promise I will go into rehab when I return." She took his word for it. He returned, went into rehab, and has been sober now for three years. Not everything went smoothly thereafter because life doesn't work that way; but they are on a good path, and she had, indeed, made the right decision, with the aid of a simple process of analyzing the benefit and the harm of her decision.

Tasks

1. When confronted with a difficult decision which will affect your earthly and spiritual life, ask yourself, What is the benefit and the harm of such a decision? If it helps, do a cost-benefit analysis. See if it helps with the decision.

2. Learn to be open and flexible. As an exercise, think of someone toward whom you have negative thoughts and feelings. Place yourself in that person's shoes. Become that person in your imagination, and allow yourself to have empathy. It may help you to cultivate a tolerance for that person, and it will certainly give you a better understanding.

3. Do not ever plan to fail, but if you do suffer a spiritual defeat, have a plan to begin again. It may be as simple as promising yourself, "Regardless of what happens in my spiritual battles, the next day I will begin anew and with confidence that the All Powerful can care for me."

Sun Tzu Said:

Whenever you station an army to observe an opponent, cut off the mountains and stay by the valleys. Watch the light; stay on the heights. When fighting on a hill, do not climb. . . . Ordinarily, an army likes high places and dislikes low ground, values light and despises darkness.

Take care of physical health and stay where there are plenty of resources. When there is no sickness in the army, it is said to be invincible. . . .

Whenever the terrain has impassable ravines, natural enclosures, natural prisons, natural traps, natural pitfalls, and natural clefts, you should leave quickly and not get near them. . . . When the trees move, the enemy is coming; when there are many blinds in the undergrowth, it is misdirection.
If birds start up, there are ambushers there.
If the animals are frightened,
there are attackers there. . . .

CHAPTER 9

Strategic
Maneuvering

Whenever traveling into unfamiliar territory, stay alert to the prospect of new spiritual opponents. Each new earthly situation brings new spiritual challenges, as well as blessings. You must remain alert and constantly aware. In determining the nature of any new terrain, watch the light as it interacts with the shadow. This will help you understand the lay of the land. In settling on new territory, stick to the high ground and avoid the low. If you settle for anything less than what you know is best for you and others, you make yourself vulnerable to attack. If you position yourself on lower ground, you may end up fighting an uphill battle, which is difficult to win. But when you have chosen the highest ground upon which to rest, if called into military action, you carry with you the momentum of the earth, as your forces descend into battle.

Generally speaking, the master warrior always seeks higher ground and avoids the low, cherishes the light and despises the darkness. This does not mean that the master warrior ignores the shadows, for when one ignores the shadows one often walks into their darkness. But there is a difference between acknowledging the darkness and embracing it. It is the difference between engaging spiritual enemies and befriending them. To know one's personal shadows and to engage them is the mark of the master combatant. To know one's personal shadows and to befriend them is to embrace the darkness and invite destruction.

The master warrior seeks earthly terrain in which spiritual sustenance is available. The master warrior maintains spiritual vitality and vigor through seeking spiritual allies, healthy friendships, and pleasant surroundings which invigorate the spirit and induce a state of inward peace. Take care to maintain good physical health as well, for the body is the foundation of the soul. A vigorous spirit relies on a healthy body to carry and support it. When there is neither spiritual nor physical sickness in master warriors, they are said to be invincible. Thomas Carlisle observed:

> Ill-health, of body or mind, is defeat. . . .
> Health alone is victory.[1]

Whenever you encounter earthly terrain which has impassible ravines, natural enclosures, traps, pitfalls, and clefts, you should vacate the area quickly and stay away from them. Metaphorically, such things can be found in places of work, recreation, relationships, and even in the home environment. When encountering such dangers one might overlook them as inconsequential to one's spiritual life, assuming they are only potential hazards which, if heeded, pose no immediate threat. But such natural hazards invite spiritual attack and place the warrior in senseless jeopardy. If your military intuition tells you that a certain situation or earthly terrain doesn't feel right, pay attention. Take action to vacate the area, for if you hesitate and are attacked, your exit will be violent, prolonged, and unnecessarily bloody.

To walk into such a precarious situation is to form friendships or business alliances with those who, because of a defect of character, bring harm to you or others. To walk into such a precarious situation is to enter an environment which rekindles your addictive compulsive behavior. To walk into such a precarious situation is to allow others to move you into circumstances beyond your control, where you can be used or even abused by another. Any situation where the people and surroundings may lead the spiritual warrior into peril is hazardous battleground and should be evacuated as quickly as possible.

In keeping an eye on the enemy, watch for his movements on the ground and for signs which indicate his advances. A veteran spiritual warrior can anticipate an enemy's movement by experience with that enemy in previous battles. You can learn from past enemy maneuvers what he will do in the future. Memorize his flanking patterns and strategy. When you see the signs, take action accordingly. If you enter terrain similar to where a battle has taken place before, be prepared to be attacked again, in the same way, and with only enough variation in enemy tactics to throw you off your guard. In entering such terrain know that if it happened once, it will happen again. The enemy is predictable on common battlegrounds. If you must traverse such terrain, stay out of the quagmires and tangled brush and search the land for potential ambush, enemy spies, and traps. Move quickly. Inaction in such circumstances invites attack and almost always brings defeat.

The following are some basic principles about scrutinizing the enemy in warfare. These principles may not only be useful for gaining strategy against spiritual opponents, but can teach the warrior how to understand the maneuvers of any opponent, whether in business, in a sporting contest, or in any of life's competitions. Study them and learn the secrets of observation in spiritual battle.

> If you know that the enemy is close and yet quiet,
> He occupies a strategic position
>
> And will attack if you remain.
> If he seems at a distance,
> And yet provokes you,
> He wants you to advance into his trap.
>
> If you find him in the open on level ground,
> He is hiding some secret military advantage.

If you sense a strong shift
In your inner being,
He is coming.

If many conflicting thoughts
Are flushed out into consciousness;
He is lying in ambush.

If feelings of dread stampede your being,
He is planning a surprise attack.

If he sends befriending messages,
Yet continues to make ready for war,
He will attack.

If he suddenly retreats in battle,
When victory was not yet decided,
He is luring you in for the kill.

If the enemy comes and goes
Haphazardly onto the battlefield,
He is weakening.

When he sends few troops
Into the subsequent rounds of battle,
He is exhausted.

When spiritual forces angrily confront you but do not go into battle, yet do not leave, you must watch them with the utmost care. You must prepare for a vigorous battle, because they will attack with force and endurance. This is the beginning of a prolonged contest which cannot be avoided. In such contests, defensive measures are called for and emphasis should be given to self-preservation. Usually in such a case there is some underlying deep-seated issue encamped in your unconscious. Perhaps you have been overwhelmed with fear in a certain circumstance, but then it disappears. You ask yourself, "Why did it come?" But more importantly, "Where did it go?"

It vanishes. You know that it stemmed from some core issue. It will return unless the core issue is resolved. A person who suffers from a phobia, for instance, may experience debilitating fear in certain circumstances, such as when in enclosed surroundings, or maybe in high places, and yet the fear retreats when the circumstance ends. The spiritual warrior must pay attention and take care. Moreover, the warrior must take action. Childhood wounds, dysfunctional conditioning, even a chemical imbalance could be the foe who will attack again with a vengeance, when similar circumstances unfold. The person needs to take these encounters seriously, and if they persist, get help from those who are qualified.

With some spiritual enemies, the best strategy is a strong defensive posture and time. If you find that you cannot defeat a certain enemy, take up a strategic defensive position where the enemy cannot defeat you. Let him deplete his own resources and weary his forces by trying. Not many spiritual forces can win a protracted battle against a well fortified opponent. Time will be the greatest factor and confer the victory. Time not only heals wounds, but it can also win battles. This is only true when caught against overwhelming odds. Do not attack an enemy that you cannot swiftly defeat, but when outnumbered, take up a defensive posture and wait it out. If you can buy enough time, you can buy victory. For instance, if you are offended or hurt by someone and know that your instinctual reaction to lash out in turn will be utterly destructive, allow yourself time to heal and forgive and that retaliatory rage will fade without bloodshed. This is true with other destructive tendencies as well. Time not only wins battles, it can also avoid them.

In spiritual warfare, it is not necessarily strength which gives the advantage. It is enough if you do not act recklessly and are able to open yourself up to a higher source of power, get a clear picture of the enemy, and find support from earthly allies. Only the one who has no plan and takes the enemy lightly is certain to be captured.

❊ *Further Application*

Remaining Alert and Constantly Aware

The attack of the spiritual enemy is most often by surprise. It is rare that the inward foe will announce its presence on the battlefield. Rather, it is usually the case that we carelessly and unmindfully trample through life oblivious to our spiritual enemies. Fear, anger, lust, guilt, depression, self-pity, insecurity, and many other such enemies use surprise as their major strategy against the well-being of our souls. Ignorant of the situations in which we often place ourselves, we set ourselves up for ambush. I know that I can slip fairly easily into naiveté and walk through life with blinders over my eyes, only to find I have inadvertently placed myself in a situation which has allowed the enemy to attack me.

One issue I have been working on is that of having appropriate emotional boundaries. People tell me I wear my emotions on my sleeves. I tend to meet someone, immediately trust them, make friends, and open my heart to them, only to find sometimes that I have misjudged their character and eventually become hurt in some way by their actions. This happened to me early in my career as I was trying to start a brand new church congregation in Chicago. I remember getting to know two particular couples who had eagerly come to the church, expressing delight at what was being offered in our church services. At the time, I heard one couple say that they have never been associated with any church for more than a year, and the other couple clearly stated that they were true seekers, never to be bound by any religious affiliation; but I let those statements pass through me as I enjoyed the glee of having two new families join our budding congregation. That's not unusual, but as I was prone to dropping all emotional guards when becoming friends, I developed a relationship with both of these couples over the next two years in which I became dependent on their physical and emotional support. One couple ran the Sunday school and nursery program, led the committee to feed the homeless, and sat on my council. The other couple adopted my wife Cathy and me, as our benevolent caretakers, not only inviting us into their home to listen to our hopes and dreams for the church and to share our struggle, but also babysitting our children and clothing them with new jackets at wintertime, taking us to dinner once a month, and becoming full confidants, as well. Since I had let down my guard completely, I was devastated when both couples announced that they were leaving the church and moving on to new horizons. They told me that it wasn't personal and that I should have known they would leave because they had practically said so in the beginning. It took my wife and me a year to recover from losing not only their physical support for the church, but more importantly, their emotional support.

Now this may be perfectly normal, but while I was licking my wounds I realized that the depth of my sorrow and depression was my own fault. I had, indeed, heard their warnings, and I ignored them. Now reflecting on their behavior throughout the two years in which they were associated with the church, I could see that there were signs all along indicating that they would leave and that I was emotionally "in too deep" to easily recover. If I had been more aware and paid attention to what these two couples were saying, as well as to my reaction to them, I would have spared myself and my church much of the grief we had to go through by simply making a few adjustments.

This is just one example of my unawareness in terms of relationships and emotional boundaries. There are many other stories I could tell, but for several years now I have worked on this problem. Instead of naively falling into a new relationship with emotional abandon, I approach potential new relationships with positive awareness. I pay attention to what is being said. One can actually learn a great deal from first impressions. I pay attention to the history of this person, as it is being told to me, and to actions and responses to my conversation. I ask myself, What does this information teach me about this person? This practice has helped me make conscious decisions regarding healthy relationships.

There are many ways to build awareness, not just in relationships, but also in knowing what circumstances may bring on the attack of a spiritual enemy. In Vietnam, the soldiers spoke of having "the thousand-yard stare," where they would train themselves to observe the distant horizon for potential ambush. People can do the same thing with their spiritual lives, by paying attention not only to what potential circumstances on the horizon may cause inner struggles, but also to their own thoughts and feelings as they traverse new territory in their lives. One way I have taught people in my spiritual warfare training to remain spiritually alert is to teach them how to become physically alert. Exercises such as sitting in the woods and meditating on the various sights and sounds one sees, or walking into a familiar room with the task of noticing something new about it, or listening to music with an ear for the different instruments, sounds, and harmonies, are all ways of building awareness. Meditating while paying special attention to your body and to where you are holding your tension—where grief is located, or fear, or peace, or joy—are also means of becoming aware of your own being. All of these exercises will help a person stay awake not only naturally but spiritually, because when one makes a habit of being aware on as many levels as possible, the spirit has a greater tendency to stay awake and alert. One can come into a mode of having a healthy spiritual "thousand-yard stare." According to Castaneda:

> The average man is aware of everything
> Only when he thinks he should be;
> The condition of the warrior, however,
> Is to be aware of everything at all times.[2]

Tasks

1. *Analyze your surroundings, both natural and spiritual. Are they healthy surroundings, creating and sustaining opportunity for spiritual growth? What changes could be made to improve your environment? Begin to make those changes today.*

2. *Learn from past mistakes. List three to five actions you took in your life that you now believe were mistakes, hindering your spiritual growth and hurting yourself and perhaps others. List three to five lessons you have learned from making such mistakes. This process will help you create future victories out of knowledge acquired from past defeats.*

3. *Involve yourself in some sort of regular physical activity or exercise. A healthy body truly helps the mind stay healthy. Take regular walks or bike excursions, join a health club, play tennis or racquetball, work out for a few minutes in your home. Any one of these or similar activities will make an incredible difference in your ability to face your spiritual foe with strength.*

Sun Tzu said:

Some terrain is easily passable; in some you get hung up. Some terrain makes for a standoff; some is narrow; some is steep; some is wide open. When both sides can come and go, the terrain is said to be easily passable. When the terrain is easily passable, take up your position first, choosing the high and sunny side, convenient to supply routes for advantage in battle. . . .

Among military forces there are those who rush, those who tarry, those who fall, those who crumble, those who riot, and those who get beaten. These are not natural disasters, but faults of the generals. . . .

Therefore, those who know martial arts do not wander when they move and do not become exhausted when they rise up. So it is said that when you know yourself and others, victory is not in danger; when you know the sky and earth, victory is inexhaustible.

CHAPTER 10

 *Traversing the Terrain*

*T*he terrain is the earth you walk while you are in this world. It is the place where you discover new countries, the context in which you fight your spiritual battles, the ground upon which you build your life and home. It is the place from which you came and the destination of all earthly beings. Thus it is written:

> In the sweat of your face
> You shall eat bread
> Till you return to the ground,
> For out of it you were taken;
> You are dust,
> And to dust you shall return.
> (Genesis 3:19)

The master warrior does not hear these words as a punishment, but as a statement of fact and even a blessing. Life is sometimes difficult, and the battles the warrior faces are real, but so are the victories and the genuine happiness which follows. The spiritual warrior is the dust of the earth, and to dust the warrior shall return, when the body no longer carries the spirit, but sleeps in the earth. We are more than sojourners on this land; we are akin to the earth and can benefit much from an awareness of this kinship.

To be one with the earth is to be one with our Mother, in all her beauty, majesty, and creative power. Therefore, know the earth, and rely upon it, even as a child relies upon its mother. Learn from the earth, even as a student learns from its teacher. Love the earth, and respect it, even as a mature adult loves and respects a parent. The master warrior is not a stranger to the earthly terrain, but becomes intimately involved with it. The spiritual warrior, though inwardly aspiring to higher planes of reality, is firmly grounded in the earth, and from it learns and obtains many things.

The earth is not remote from the spirit. Though separated in dimension, the spirit rests within the earth, and the earth is its image. Therefore, the master warrior acquires knowledge of all types of terrain, to gain strategic advantage when in battle and to seek and find rest in its beauty and solitude in times of peace. Acquiring the earth as an ally, the master warrior is always at home, never completely alone, and has continual support, no matter how distant the journey or how remote the battlefield. The earth, sun, moon, and stars are never farther away than just beneath the feet and above the head.

In preparation for spiritual warfare, listen to the earth, the wind, the trees, and the birds of the air. In the most ancient days, nature was the revelation of the true spiritual warriors. Though many revelations have since been written and many truths are contained within them, the Divine has not stopped speaking in this first and most original voice. God created this earth, and God's image is upon it. God can be seen within it and communicates through it. Therefore, it has been said:

> Every created thing is by nature a receiver of God.
> It is able to do this because it was created in God by God;
> And because it was created in this way,
> It is an analogue and is like an image of God in a mirror.[1]

The wind sings a different song each day, according to the changing climate and heavenly conditions. The trees whisper their message according to the wind and its melody. The birds come and go with the wind and utter their communications from tree to whispering tree. Each has its own message, and each message is different from day to day and at each moment of the day. To the nonobservant, these songs seem unrelated and irrelevant. To the spiritual warrior, they are so many signs and symbols stirring the warrior's thoughts and awareness. The master combatants of old, not being cut off from their surroundings, could discriminate the varying messages of their melodies. Some would affirm a spiritual path well chosen. Some would cry out a warning that the enemy is near and to go another way. Some would offer cheer and consolation. Some would honor. Some would scoff and scold to initiate deeper thought and self-reflection. To many ancient warriors, the animals themselves were messengers from the Divine. Whether encountered on a journey or seen in a dream, they offered help, companionship, and secret knowledge for the warrior to use in impending battle.

Though the inner winds of doubt blow heavily upon the warrior spirit of today, the softer melodies offering insight and wisdom may still stir the warrior heart. The trees continue to whisper, and the birds sing as they did in ancient times. Learn to quiet the thoughts between battles and to calm the emotions which deafen spiritual hearing and perception. Be still in the forest and fields of the earthly terrain, and listen. Listen and observe. You will hear with your ears and see with your eyes, but it will be your heart which will receive and understand. Reunite with the world around you, and you can face the winds of doubt and march with the strength of a thousand allies against the spiritual oppressor, with the force of the earth and the wisdom of the heavens. Thus in solitude and humility, you will call out to your allies in the earth, even as Black Elk cried out:

> Hear me, four quarters of the world—
> A relative I am!
> Give me the strength to walk the soft earth,
> A relative to all that is!
> Give me the eyes to see and the strength to understand,

That I may be like you.
With your power only can I face the winds.[2]

Though nature can be an ally in battle, the spiritual warrior travels on many kinds of earthly terrain which offer a variety of challenges. Every new situation, every encounter, every twist of fate, and every new endeavor bring new ground for the warrior to traverse. Many of these are grounds for inward battles, as each situation produces its own challenges and predicaments. There are spiritual battles to be fought and spiritual wars to be won. The master combatant masters the terrain, and in so doing, masters the battle.

Regarding spiritual warfare, there are generally six kinds of battle terrain: the accessible; that which entangles; that which leads to a stalemate; that which is narrow; that which is steep; and that which is wide open. Understanding these six types of terrain is of the utmost importance.

1. Accessible terrain is that on which you can easily move into and out of battle, by changing circumstances and conditions of day-to-day life. For example, if you choose to tackle laziness by working more diligently at the office, or to be nicer to coworkers, you move on accessible terrain. You go into this battle by choice, and you come out by choice. You can move freely and have a free hand to change your behavior.

2. Terrain which entangles describes situations where you find yourself in a battle you did not expect and which proves to be hard to escape. Finding yourself in a sexually charged relationship with someone other than your spouse is, for example, fighting on terrain which entangles. This is especially true if it is someone you must work with on a regular basis.

3. Stalemating terrain seems to give no advantage to you or to your spiritual foe. On it, you do not lose ground but cannot seem to gain ground. For instance, you work to clean up your language, or your wandering thoughts, and though it doesn't seem to get any worse, it doesn't get any better. It is a standoff.

4. When the path is narrow, you have a clear understanding of the direction you must go, but not many choices of how to get there. There seems only one way—straight ahead. You must press forward no matter how daunting the appearance of the inward foe who is blocking you. For instance, the path is narrow when the only way to heal yourself is to break off an unhealthy relationship, or when one's addictive behavior calls for abstinence from the substance abused. There is only one solution and it must be followed. It is the only way to gain ground.

5. On steep ground, when you occupy the higher position, the battle often turns in your favor, because the earth favors you. However, when the enemy carries the force of the earth, rushing down upon your forces, you will be overrun. Warriors who find themselves in circumstances where they are seduced, duped, or tricked into destructive behavior have fallen on steep ground. If you are overwhelmed, learn from your mistakes in your positioning for battle, and move on. If ambushed in such circumstances, do not deplete your strength or your resolve with shame. The situation could not be avoided. If it happens repeatedly, leave the territory altogether. You are not paying attention to the lay of the land.

6. On a wide open field for battle, when circumstances produce many opportunities for advance and yet many opportunities for misfortune, it is not advantageous to challenge a spiritual foe. The direction is not yet clear. Wait in a defensive posture until the situation defines itself, or until attacked. This strategy leaves the enemy with the unfortunate choice of closing his own options while leaving yours intact. It is like the parable of the farmer who found that his enemy had sown tares with the farmer's young wheat. The farmer did not remove the tares until they were grown and so could be clearly seen and removed without hurting the wheat. In the same way, the spiritual warrior must wait until the enemy has committed to his plans and made his position known. For some, this is called "hitting bottom," if not in actuality, then in imagination.

Then the enemy can be confronted and uprooted in battle. As Lao Tzu taught:

> If you want to shrink something,
> You must first allow it to expand.
> If you want to get rid of something,
> You must first allow it to flourish.[3]

So among spiritual warriors, there are those who rush and those who tarry, those who fall and those who crumble, those who are in chaos and those who get beaten. These are not natural disasters, but rather the faults of the warriors themselves.

Those who have the power to defeat a certain spiritual enemy, but only use a portion of their forces, are in a rush. Those who are emotionally strong, but weak in their decision making, tarry. Those who are quick to make decisions, but whose will is weak, fall. Those who act impulsively in dealing with the spiritual enemy, carelessly engaging one and then another without strategy, will crumble. Those who are morally weak and lax, practicing no spiritual discipline and having no focus on the spiritual enemy, soon find themselves in chaos. Those who cannot gauge the strength of their spiritual enemies, and who do not know their own strengths and weaknesses, are the ones who are spiritually beaten.

These are six ways to certain spiritual defeat. They are the spiritual warrior's utmost responsibility and must be thoroughly examined.

The earthly terrain is a kin and an ally, in life and in spiritual battle. To know the earth, to become aware of the challenges and the benefits of the battle terrain, to assess the enemy's situation on the terrain and create conditions that lead to victory, is the way of the superior military combatant. The one who fights with full knowledge of these factors is certain to win; the one who fights without it is certain to lose.

Therefore, when those who understand spiritual warfare move, they do not go the wrong way, and when they take action, they do not reach a dead end. Remember these words of Sun Tzu:

> If you know the other and know yourself,
> Victory will not be at risk;
> If you know the earth and know the sky,
> Victory can be total.

❋ Further Application

Acquiring the Earth as an Ally

One of my early childhood memories is the time when I spent one of my first weekends away from home at a friend's summer house in the Catskill mountains. By the second night, I became conspicuously homesick. My friend had an older sister, Liz, who had been babysitting and playing games with us during the weekend. She noticed how timid and withdrawn I was becoming and asked me if I was homesick. When I nodded affirmatively, she beckoned me to come outside with her under the evening sky. As we stood under the stars she told me that she used to get homesick a lot. Her family had moved several times because of her dad's job, and she'd always miss so much the place she had left behind. Then she asked me to look up to the stars. She said, "When I became lonely I'd always come outside and look up at these stars. I think of them as my friends. They are always there to greet me, no matter where I am. I can be across the country and when I look up at these stars, they tell me I'm still at home." Her words did give me some comfort then, but I had no idea how important they would become to me in time.

Through growing up in the woods, hunting in the snowy mountains of Pennsylvania, gaining an appreciation of the Native American outlook, and my own upbringing in the Swedenborgian religion—which teaches that nature is a mirror in which one can behold the face of God—I've grown to see and deeply sense that the natural world is not only my home but a friend and ally in my spiritual struggles. God created the world of nature in such a way that it can support us, nurture us, teach us, and reveal to us the presence and care of God.

I came to this fundamental way of perceiving nature by spending a good deal of time in it and familiarizing myself with its workings. I recommend this practice to anyone who is endeavoring to live in spirit and integrity. When one can come to the sense that he or she is not an alien to the natural world, but very much akin to it, then the real lessons begin. For me, those lessons and the sense of help I receive do not come through my head but through my heart. I learned this through the mentoring of a good friend and expert tracker, Jerry Finkeldey. I asked him, "How do I learn from nature? I can see that nature can teach me so many things, but I can't seem to understand what is being taught." He told me bluntly, "Get out of your head. The earth speaks through a different voice. You have to listen with different hearing. Hear from your heart." This lesson has struck home with me many times since our conversation. I began to make a practice of getting out into the quiet of nature, especially under times of stress at work. When my mind would begin to spin and I would lose touch with my Creator and the sense of the purpose of my existence, I knew it was time to head to the woods. I'd look for a quiet spot, sit down, and simply absorb what was happening around me. Through the practice of observing nature with my heart, I quickly found that the message being absorbed by my whole being was one of peace and centeredness. As the squirrels and chipmunks, deer, and birds of all kinds reappeared in close proximity to me, sensing I was their kin, I experienced the message of Mother Earth on a cellular level: "All is right in God's world. You are in the perfect place at the perfect time." Through returning to nature, especially in an effort to regroup from my spiritual battles and to renew my strength, I have found an ally and kin. And no matter where I may be, I can always look up to the sky, or feel the ground under my feet, and know that my ally is with me.

Tasks

1. *Become connected with the earth. Find a place in nature, even if you must travel to get there. Sit quietly and alone, and listen. Do not let your mind drift into daydreaming, but keep alert. Scan the horizon with your eyes, look into the trees and sky, and observe intently. All the while allow nature to speak to you and to flow into you with her gentle rhythms. At first, feel the peace. With much practice, sense the vast meaning of what you hear, feel, and see. If you are able, make visits to nature a habit.*

2. *Pay attention to the birds and animals which present themselves to you, whether this be in nature, in magazines, or on television. They are symbols and representatives of things spiritual. If you find that there are some particular birds, animals, or symbols which appear on a regular basis, learn about these things; study them. What do they come to mean to you? Notice what part they play in your life and how your relationship with them grows.*

3. *Learn to know yourself: write a brief description of the noble you. Know your enemy: write a brief description of the destructive tendencies which attack your life and well-being. How do these two relate to each other? Any insights?*

Sun Tzu Said:

   According to the rule for military operations, there are nine kinds of ground. Ground where local interests fight among themselves on their own territory is called a "ground of dissolution." When you enter others' land, but not deeply, you are on "light ground." Land that would be advantageous to whomever won it is called "ground of contention." Land on which you and others can come and go is called a "trafficked ground." Land surrounded on three sides by competitors which would give the winner of it access to all the people on the continent is called "intersecting ground." Where you have entered deeply into others' land, past many cities and towns, is called "heavy ground." Where you traverse mountain forests, steep defiles, marshes, or any route difficult to travel is called "bad ground." Where the way in is narrow and the way out is circuitous, so a small enemy force can strike you, even though your numbers are greater, is called "surrounded ground." When you will survive if you fight quickly and perish if you do not, you are on "dying ground."

Battlegrounds

There are many kinds of battlegrounds on which you will face the spiritual foe: (1) scattering ground, (2) marginal ground, (3) contested ground, (4) strategically vital ground, (5) difficult ground, (6) ground where you are vulnerable to ambush, and (7) deadly ground.

1. Scattering ground: The spiritual warrior enters scattering ground when confronted with a situation which divides the mind and blurs the intentions, thus scattering thoughts in all different directions. Faced with choices, all of which seem of equal importance, the spiritual warrior becomes paralyzed into nonaction. This truth is illustrated in the Hebrew story of Elijah, who witnessed the children of Israel caught between the worship of Baal and the local gods who were supposed to bring abundance and good fortune and their allegiance to Yahweh, the God who had led them every step of their journey. Wounded from indecision, they hobbled back and forth between these two opposite polls, unable to decide to whom to swear allegiance. Thus Elijah taunted them, "How long will you limp between two opinions?" (1 Kings 18:21) As long as we are reluctant to choose between actions, we will remain on scattering ground. For instance, a person caught in a dysfunctional relationship because he or she measures the good things about it as equal to the bad, remains on such ground.

2. Marginal ground: To fight on marginal ground is to take up a sword in defense of what is nonessential. It is to waste valuable time and initiative on an insignificant spiritual foe, when a larger and more significant spiritual foe continues to rain down his aggression upon you and within you. It has been described as straining out a gnat, but swallowing a camel. It is to occupy oneself with trivia in order to avoid the call to a greater battle and thus to the potential of new freedom. I have seen this trait especially with the clergy and in academic arenas, where some become caught up in great arguments about how many angels can dance on the head of a pin, while worlds burn down around them. It is an escape from reality and constitutes denial to focus on intellectual trivia, even about one's life, and to hide from issues of personal accountability, change, hard work, and love. Every warrior must ask, "Am I fighting for something essential, or am I wasting my time with trivia?"

3. *Contested ground* is that on which the spiritual warrior fights for new territory and to change behavior from destructive to beneficial and life-giving. It is a battle which the spiritual enemy fights with a fury, for once the victory is achieved, the enemy is banished from that particular field. It is a struggle for ownership of the immediate earthly terrain. Giving up a bad habit or learning to forgive someone are battles which take place on contested ground.

4. *Strategically vital ground:* Spiritual warriors find themselves fighting for strategically vital ground when placed in a situation in which they must change impulses, thought patterns, and behaviors or they will lose more ground than they have gained. If they do not bring down their spiritual opponent, they will suffer greatly, even to the point of losing the love of others, or their reputation, usefulness, or even earthly employment. Thus the battle becomes strategically vital for their continuing journey and well-being. Those fighting addiction and compulsive behavior do battle on this ground.

5. *Difficult ground:* To fight on difficult ground is to attempt to vanquish a spiritual enemy in difficult circumstances.

It involves finding oneself in a situation where movements are restricted, choices are limited, and pitfalls are prevalent. These are often inner skirmishes where the spiritual warrior has no clear choice of action and where any decision seems to leave something to be desired. However, some decision is called for in order to avoid an even worse disaster.

6. Ground vulnerable to ambush is dangerous ground. To enter this ground is to place oneself in positions open to spiritual attack. It means carelessly entering enemy territory without a plan of assault. In such circumstances, the spiritual warrior becomes surrounded by enemies and may find it difficult to escape. This happens when a spiritual warrior enters into situations which are prone to waken inner destructive tendencies, which then assault without restraint. It involves making choices, creating scenarios, and forming relationships which become dangerous to spiritual life and well-being.

7. Deadly ground: Ground upon which you will only survive spiritually if you fight with all your might is deadly ground. It describes a time when the spiritual warrior has no choice but to fight with every ounce of strength and purpose to defeat a spiritual foe, or the result is spiritual death. It is a real life-and-death struggle in the spiritual realm. This is a time when the spiritual warrior faces a clear choice between serving the purposes of evil or the purposes of good, between choosing the darkness or the light.

Knowing these battlegrounds, pay attention to the following:

Let there be no battle on scattering ground; back out and look more carefully at the situation until choices become more clear.

Let there be no lingering on marginal ground; face the true enemy and experience true victory.

Let there be steadfastness on contested ground; if new territory can be won, peace can come to new regions.

On strategically vital ground form alliances, for the battle is too great to fight it alone, and the stakes are too high not to ask for aid.

On difficult ground press ahead; the sooner you can pass through to better ground, the less opportunity for disaster.

Avoid ground vulnerable to ambush; if accidentally entering such terrain, exit it as soon as possible. If surrounded, plot an escape.

When on deadly ground, there is only one alternative: fight.

Hence, the psychology of the spiritual warrior is to resist when surrounded, fight when it cannot be avoided, and obey higher commands when in danger.

Spiritual warfare is such that the supreme consideration is action. This is the key to keeping the spiritual enemy from seizing and holding ground within your life and being. Keep the enemy guessing your every move and thus on the defensive. Act swiftly, and you can stay ahead of the enemy on battlegrounds which produce the strategic advantage. Spiritual change which leads to victory takes place through action and nothing else. In spiritual warfare, take the risk of action. Sir Walter Scott saw this clearly:

One hour of life,
Crowded to the full with glorious action,
And filled with noble risks,
Is worth whole years
Of those mean observances of paltry decorum.[1]

In general, the further you penetrate into enemy territory, routing the spiritual foe, the stronger your resolve becomes and the more focused your purpose. The further you penetrate into enemy territory, the more sustenance is discovered along the way. Plunder the surrounding fields and you will have ample provisions. It is important that you care for yourself while on your journey, especially when crossing into enemy territory and taking new ground for spiritual life. Though you will encounter new battles, there will be times of peace and rejuvenation. Nourish yourself with light-heartedness and pleasure. Keep comforting words of hope in your mind and heart. Ponder them. Rest between battles and take delight in your victories. Care for your body and your soul, and both will lead you to paths of victory and consolation. If entering enemy terrain, do your best if called to battle, but do not pine away in sorrow if defeated. Learn from defeat, and prepare for another day and for another battle toward victory. Say to your enemy what has been said by spiritual warriors of old:

> Do not rejoice against me,
> O my enemy:
> If I fall,
> I shall arise.
> (Micah 7:8)

Therefore, on all battlegrounds, let the heart remain steadfast in the mission at hand and the mind remain focused on victory.

❋ *Further Application*

Forming Alliances

When on strategically vital ground form alliances, for the battle is too great to fight it alone, and the stakes are too high not to ask for aid. Having worked with men on men's issues for over a decade, as well as with various recovery and spiritual growth groups, I know how easy it is for everyone, but especially men, to isolate themselves when it comes to suffering through spiritual battle. Men have often been raised with the idea that they must internalize their pain, hide it from their peers lest they manifest weakness and vulnerability, and fight alone. In my work with men I try to show them that their secret battles are not so unique and that help in the way of spiritual allies and mentors is waiting for them if only they will reach out with trust. One way I have driven this point home in seminars is to ask all two or three hundred men to close their eyes and get in touch with their pain. I have them hold their hands on their hearts and repeat silently to themselves, "I am alone." I ask them to get in touch with this loneliness if it is within them. I then ask if they believe this is secret knowledge that only they are feeling. Would they like to see that other men may share in what they are feeling and may have the ability to help? With their eyes closed, I ask them to raise their hands if they feel that loneliness and are willing to reach out. I then ask them to open their eyes and look around. There isn't a man in the room without his hand up, and the secret of inner distress is not a secret anymore. They realize they are not alone and that they can begin to reach out to other men.

Women seem to form alliances much more easily and be willing to reach out to other women, exposing their need and vulnerability. But regardless of our sex, forming alliances—in the way of support groups, mentors, special friendships based on spiritual principles—helps the spiritual warrior immensely. Telling my story in the context of a shared desire for personal integrity and growth helps me not only understand myself better, but holds me accountable to someone other than myself. I can lie to myself, but it is harder to lie to eight or nine other people about my spiritual foibles and my struggles with them. I know that when I hear other people speaking from the heart about their struggles—listening to their stories of defeat, their grief and fears, their hopes and aspirations, their inner child and their shadow self—I feel a sense of healing taking place within myself. I not only realize that they are telling my story, but I believe that it is the empathy I feel for them that brings me healing. That sense that we are all one in our struggles, and sharing that oneness heals us and allows us to move forward with the changes that need to take place in our spiritual lives.

Anyone can benefit from joining a group of people willing to dedicate themselves to a spiritual discipline or path, whether that be a twelve-step group, a spiritual warrior group, or a generic support group for spiritual life. For those who are struggling on strategically vital ground, where defeat means the difference between life or death, personal success or failure, the essential question to ask oneself is, "Can I afford not to have allies in my struggle?" The answer for many who suffer from immense and powerful spiritual enemies is clear—relying on spiritual allies for support may be the only key to victory. It has worked for millions in twelve-step and other support groups throughout the world, and it will work for you.

Tasks

1. *Study the different kinds of battlegrounds described in this chapter. Reflecting on your life, are there particular kinds of terrain upon which you find yourself fighting most of your inward battles? Is there a reason for this pattern? Is it beneficial to you or harmful? What steps can you take to make necessary changes in your strategic positioning?*

2. *One of the greatest barriers to spiritual growth is inaction. Reflect on your spiritual condition. Is there an area in your life where you are at a stalemate with your spiritual enemy? Choose*

an appropriate action to reengage that enemy with determination. Begin that action immediately. Notice how quickly it can make a difference.

3. *Focus your purpose. Take time to determine the exact nature of what you would like to do and be in life. Make it as concrete a picture as possible. List some goals to reach that objective. Take action to achieve them.*

Sun Tzu said:

There are five kinds of fire attack: burning people, burning supplies, burning equipment, burning storehouses, and burning weapons. . . . Armies must know there are adaptations of these five kinds of fire attack and adhere to them scientifically.

—Sun Tzu

CHAPTER 12

Spiritual Fire

*F*ire is used as a weapon of war. This is also true in spiritual warfare, but it is spiritual fire which is used in battle. Spiritual fire is the flame of love. When used by the enemy it becomes the flame of the love for self, material possessions, self-indulgence, lust, and self-gratification. In its most destructive form, this spiritual fire turns to hatred and its devouring qualities. The forces of evil use this fire to burn down the bulwarks of virtue and morality, to incinerate lovingkindness, empathy, and mercy. It is a weapon to be feared, for it can consume the very marrow of the mind and soul, leaving the spiritual warrior nothing more than an empty and charred shell of a human being. Care must be taken not to allow the enemy to approach with such fire. When fires of this nature are ignited by the enemy within the encampment of the spiritual warrior's soul and being, every effort must be made to extinguish them immediately, for they can grow rapidly out of control, producing incredible damage.

But there is another kind of fire which is not hurtful. It is a fire that does not consume or take away life. It is a fire which warms, rejuvenates, and gives life and meaning to all things in the spiritual warrior's world. It is the fire of love.

Love can be defined in many ways. It is the very life of everything that lives and breathes. It is the force that lives and moves in all things. It is the motivating force for good in the spiritual warrior. It is what causes the spiritual warrior to dream of victory and peace and a better way of life for all. It is the inspiration which moves the spiritual warrior to charge courageously into the abyss to fight the spiritual foe, and it is love which brings ultimate victory and the lasting fruits of victory. Love is a desire to serve and a heartfelt passion to give what is one's own, on all levels, to another, to provide for the happiness of others, and to bless. Love is the very life of the spiritual warrior. As it is written:

> If I speak in the tongues of men and of angels,
> But have not love,
> I am a noisy gong or a clanging cymbal.
> And if I have prophetic powers,
> And understand all the mysteries and all knowledge,
> And if I have all faith,
> So as to remove mountains,
> But have not love,
> I am nothing.
> If I give away all I have,
> And if I deliver my body to be burned,
> But have not love,
> I gain nothing.
> Love is patient and kind;
> Love is not jealous or boastful;
> It is not arrogant or rude.
> Love does not insist on its own way;
> It is not irritable or resentful;
> It does not rejoice at wrong,
> But rejoices in the right.
> Love bears all things,
> Believes all things,
> Hopes all things,
> Endures all things.
> Love never ends.
>   (1 Corinthians 13:1-8)

In spiritual battle, it is love which is most often attacked. The forces of darkness detest what the spiritual warrior loves the most and strike with a fury to extinguish this greatest weapon of spiritual life. The forces of darkness rage against love and battle against it with hatred and determination. For if love can be conquered, all can be conquered; if love can be destroyed, all can be destroyed. However, the power of love is as infinite and omnipotent as its Source. It is love which endures to the end, and it is love which conquers all spiritual foes.

The spiritual warrior need not be alarmed when the core of one's being and all that one truly cares for is assaulted by deadly forces. It is not evidence of a defective gap in the spiritual warrior's battle array, nor evidence of an ill-prepared strategy. It does not signify good intentions gone bad, or the discovery of misguided aspiration for a better life. What one loves, whether it is humanity, freedom for all people, a partner or a child, justice, mercy, righteousness, or peace—this love is what the enemy attacks. Yet it is this love which gives the spiritual warrior the fortitude to endure the struggle even to the end, when victory is achieved. For as a weapon, love, like water, is the gentlest of all substances, and yet it conquers all in its own way and time. Lao Tzu observed:

> Nothing in the world
> Is as soft and yielding as water.
> Yet for dissolving the hard and inflexible,
> Nothing can surpass it.

> The soft overcomes the hard;
> The gentle overcomes the rigid.
> Everyone knows this is true,
> But few can put it into practice.[1]

Love is put into practice by the removal of hate and condemnation, through ejecting the desire to dominate over others and to serve only the self. Remove the barriers to love, and it flows freely into consciousness and into life. It flows into acts of kindness, in giving, in forgiveness and mercy, in being of useful service, and in standing up for and defending what is spiritually precious to all. It becomes the core of courage in the spiritual warrior. It enables the spiritual warrior to believe in and fight for a cause greater than self, to face the door of death, and to step through to new life. There are four basic loves:

Love for self
Love for the material world
Love for others
Love for the Divine

These four loves exist in all spiritual warriors and, when properly ordered, bring happiness and spiritual life. When out of order, they invite enemy attack. These loves are out of order when the love for self reigns supreme in the spiritual warrior's life and actions, for all actions are taken for self-promotion and care. These loves are out of order when the spiritual warrior holds material gain as the greatest prize, for this closes the vertical pathway to spirituality and cuts off communication with the Source. Even when the love of others reigns over all, without regard for the Divine, the spiritual warrior becomes a servant to others, and a dependence upon other's approval cripples the warrior's ability to walk the genuine spiritual path. The Tao Te Ching reminds us:

If you look to others for fulfillment,
You will never truly be fulfilled.[2]

The warrior serves the King, not the people. The spiritual warrior serves the Divine and the cause of the Divine. When rightly ordered, love for the Divine reigns within the expert combatant, followed by a love for others as a servant to this greater love, followed in turn by a love and respect for the material world and, finally, for self. When this order is accomplished, the spiritual warrior is perfected and stands as a noble warrior and master combatant. Positioned upon such a foundation, the warrior cannot be moved by the enemy.

Though love is attacked by the spiritual enemy, it is through the struggle of combat that love is purified. It grows and is perfected. Wading through the smoke of spiritual warfare, goals become clearer. Pushing through enemy lines in the heat of such war, devotion becomes stronger. Enduring the toil of such war, the spiritual warrior's power becomes a mighty force for good. Suffering the pain of spiritual warfare, the joy becomes ever so sweet. Therefore, continue your campaign in the confusion of battle, and do not fail to penetrate the enemy lines in the heat of combat. Endure until the end, knowing that through such struggle what is weak becomes mighty and the anguish of battle will give way to the ecstasy of triumph.

�֍ *Further Application*

Love Conquers All Spiritual Foes

In spiritual battle, it is love which is most often attacked. However, it is love which endures to the end, and it is love which conquers all spiritual foes. In my years of pastoring and counseling others, I have seen countless men and women come to me in distress because they believe they are not good people and that their spiritual enemies have defeated them. They say so because they have grown acutely aware of their spiritual enemies who seem to assault everything they love, whether that be their love for their spouse, children, being of useful service to others, or walking with integrity. They feel that because they are in states of temptation or spiritual battle, they must be wrong or evil. The first thing I tell them is that their worry about it is a very good sign. People confirmed in a life of evil or disorder don't go through temptation or battle. They just act on their destructive tendencies. Concern over one's spiritual condition, on the other hand, is often the beginning of one's rebirth and growth.

Emanuel Swedenborg taught in his books about the battle between the devils and angels over the human soul that the devils attack what we love most. They attack mutual love, integrity, and righteousness; since they are evil, they can't stand these things. While the devils attack, the angels protect what we love; through the struggle which ensues and the choices we make between good and evil, our love is strengthened as we face the challenges against it. Whether you believe in devils and angels is your business, but the principle is sound. Ask yourself, "If I didn't care about my marriage, why would I be battling the temptation to walk away from it? If I didn't care about my daughter, why would I struggle to approach her with maturity and calm rather than the rage I so often feel in my heart? If I didn't care about walking with integrity, would I even struggle to do so?" The answer is that the enemy, whether we call it the shadow self, demons, or devils, attacks the most noble part of us in an effort to bring us down. Knowing this truth, we find comfort in it. We still need to struggle against such attacks, but the struggle is a sign not of weakness but of strength. The attacks are not necessarily times of certain downfall or erosion of character, but opportunities for commitment and growth, and character builders. The wonderful thing about victory in spiritual battle is not simply that we fend off an enemy to our well-being and potential for growth, but that by fending off that enemy, we grow.

Tasks

1. *Anger and resentment block lovingkindness and its healing power. Are fires of anger and resentment lingering in your being? Can you take steps toward forgiveness and let go of the anger? Allow those destructive fires to die out. Notice the relief and the peace which follow.*

2. *Notice what is being attacked in your life and the spiritual battles you are thrust into. By careful examination, can you see that it is something you truly love which is being attacked? Remind yourself that spiritual struggle does not indicate weakness but strength. Pray for strength in the areas of battle and for victory.*

3. *Love in action brings spiritual transformation. Think of some people who could benefit from an act of kindness. Write their names on a list. Beside those names, write down an action you could take to brighten their day and experience some of your kindness. This could be a phone call, a note of appreciation, an offer of help, an anonymous gift—whatever you think would be appropriate. Within the week, perform those kind actions. See how it helps them and see how it helps you.*

Sun Tzu said:

What enables an intelligent government and a wise military leadership to overcome others and achieve extraordinary accomplishments is foreknowledge. . . .

So only a brilliant ruler or a wise general who can use the highly intelligent for espionage is sure of great success. This practice is essential for military operations, and the armies depend on it in their actions.

The Way of the Warrior

 T he way of the warrior begins not with the individual but with the Divine. The way of the Divine is the way of life—the way of ever creating anew and sustaining, at all times, what has been created. It is the continual nourishing of all things, through incomprehensible love, inconceivable wisdom, and immeasurable ability. What the Divine confers on each created entity is priceless in its value and so full of meaning that it is beyond the full scope of perception. It is described in so many words: love, mercy, compassion, truth, justice, wisdom. Yet these are human terms which describe reflections of divine action, but not the Divine itself, which is unknowable. However, it is through these reflections that the spiritual warrior learns from the Source of all that is. It is through opening up to the way of divine life that the spiritual warrior is created anew, sustained, animated, enlightened, empowered, and directed. Through this process the master spiritual com-batant walks in the Way and becomes a reflection of the Way. Thus it is a state of being and a state of doing. As the warriors of old declared:

> To you, O Lord, I lift up my soul.
> O my God, I trust in you,
> Let me not be put to shame;
> Do not let my enemies exult over me. . . .
> Show me your ways . . .
> Teach me your paths.
> Lead me in your truth, and teach me,

For you are the God of my salvation;
For you I wait all the day long.
(Psalm 25:1-5)

The spiritual warrior cannot enter into this divine way except through conscious commitment. This is the cause which motivates and directs the spiritual warrior. Through this cause, which can best be summed up as an allegiance to what is good and true, the warrior is able to transcend self. Through right being and action, as a result of such transcendence, the spiritual warrior is transformed. This transformation has been called many names: rebirth, spirituality, recovery, and salvation. It is, for the spiritual warrior, the realization of complete and total victory. Therefore, if you wish to become a master warrior, you must form an allegiance to what is good and true. In being, thought, and action, this is your cause and one for which you will fight. This is your cause and one for which you will, if necessary, die.

When such a noble cause is adopted, the battle begins. Though every victory over the dark forces brings freedom, new light and love, and new humanity to all who dwell on the earthly terrain, it begins within. It must necessarily begin within. A spiritual warrior cannot change the world if the warrior cannot change self. A spiritual warrior cannot rid the world of evil if the warrior is unable to rid himself of evil. A spiritual warrior is hard pressed to contribute goodness and love to the world if the warrior is unable to produce goodness and love in oneself. The battle begins within. And yet, through victory within, there comes victory without. Through ejecting the demons within one's own conscious battlefields, such demons are cast out of the world. Through the cultivation of lovingkindness, understanding, and mercy in oneself, the world receives as much in turn. Therefore, fight the battle within, and you fight for the fulfillment of the noble cause in both worlds. Win the battle, and it is victory for one and the many. In the *Way of the Peaceful Warrior*, Dan Millman writes:

When you become fully responsible
 for your life,
You can become fully human;
Once you become human,
You may discover what it means
To be a warrior.[1]

As the spiritual enemies within are encountered, either
through self-discovery or attack, the way of the master warrior
is one of calm, determination, persistence, humility, and openness to divine leading. Without calm there can be no openness;
without determination there can be no persistence; without
humility there can be no divine leading; without divine leading
there can be no spiritual victory. One depends upon the other;
as soldiers in battle, they rely upon each other. When in the heat
of battle, do not hesitate to call for spiritual aid. It is the key to
winning every combat. When all seems lost, continue in your
determination. The tide of battle will turn. If it does not turn,
and defeat is inevitable, rather than surrendering in lost hope to
the enemy, surrender to the Divine. Victory is never impossible,
only sometimes delayed. Remember that with the Divine, all
things are possible, always. Victory is achievable, always.

To him who overcomes
I will give some of the hidden manna to eat.
And I will give him a white stone,
And on the stone a new name written
Which no one knows except him who receives it.
                    (Revelation 2:17)

Through victory in spiritual battle, the warrior grows
in power, strength, and ability, in wisdom and in vitality. The
battles which ensue in the course of time may be as fierce as
ever, but the warrior's powers and abilities are as strong and
keen as ever. Through such engagements the master warrior
learns the terrain, avoids the deadly, makes camp on protected

ground, and sets up battle array to ensure strategic advantage. Through right disposition, skill in maneuvering, awareness of the types of battlegrounds, the quality of the enemy, and one's own strengths and weaknesses, the master warrior becomes invincible against spiritual enemies. Freed from the enemy, the master warrior walks in the Way. It is the Way of life and the Way of love. It is a sacred Way, one with the Divine, akin to all that is, experienced by the self, and witnessed by all. As Black Elk spoke of this sacred Way:

> With visible breath I am walking.
> A voice I am sending as I walk.
> In a sacred manner I am walking.
> With visible tracks I am walking.
> In a sacred manner I walk.[2]

Because of what the spiritual warrior has seen and experienced in battle, having become fully aware of spiritual and earthly terrains, the warrior sees a thousand yards ahead of most people. Walking softly upon the terrain, awake to all things, the spiritual warrior scans the horizon with precision and care, as alert as an eagle, as careful as a deer, as quiet as a fox. The warrior sees what others do not see, acts while others react, knows while others are still only guessing. Because of the scars of previous battles, the spiritual warrior walks in humility, open to all things and to all beings. Because of the memory of the pain of battle, the spiritual warrior has deep empathy for all who are struggling against their own personal demons. Experiencing the isolation of spiritual combat, the master warrior offers a hand and companionship to those crying out for spiritual allies.

The spiritual warrior seeks out fellow combatants to bond in support of one another, to unite as allies against a common foe. Master warriors aid one another in battle, not that they fight each other's battles, but rather that they offer understanding, encouragement, wisdom, and support. Thich Nhat Hanh teaches us:

> My well-being, my happiness
> Depends very much on you,
> And your well-being, your happiness,
> Depends on me.
> I am responsible for you,
> And you are responsible for me.
> Anything I do wrong,
> You will suffer,
> And anything you do wrong,
> I have to suffer.
> Therefore,
> In order to take care of you,
> I have to take care of myself.[3]

United together in a common cause, they enter the greater war to turn the tide from falling darkness to emerging light. Because of this unity, they are blessed. Therefore, it is said:

> God loves those who fight for his cause
> In the ranks as firm as a mighty edifice.
> (Koran 61:3)

Bonded together in love and in God's blessing, the ultimate victory can be achieved, and spirituality can be restored to all.

This is the battle, the cause for which each spiritual warrior fights. There is no battle more noble. This is the art of spiritual warfare, and the guide to victory. It cannot be achieved in any other way. Therefore, go forward in this cause, with courage and in the name of your God. May your spiritual battles end in triumph. May you find lasting peace. In your last days, may you rest content in your ways; and entering into the full joy of spiritual victory, may you declare with a satisfied heart:

> I have fought the good fight,
> I have finished the race.
> I have kept the faith.
>
> (2 Timothy 4:7)

❋ Further Application

Gaining Power Through Victory

Through victory in spiritual battle, the warrior grows in power, strength, ability, wisdom, and vitality. One of the greatest blessings in my life has been to play a role in helping people access the noble warrior within and to overcome their spiritual enemies. To witness the miracles that take place in people's lives, as they find inner peace for the first time, experience measurable growth in character, learn discipline, and enjoy the growing wisdom of walking with spirit and integrity, is unmatched in its reward. I remember well not only the words, but the faces and the voices filled with gratitude, as so many have recounted the blessings they have received from taking the Spiritual Warfare Effectiveness Training courses and retreats. One man confessed that he had been battling depression all of his life and that somehow, for the first time, he was able to understand this enemy to confront it, and to be free from its grasp. Another spoke of the fading fear, of how the power of his enemy faded as the illusions faded, and of how he now walks without looking over his shoulder for this enemy to emerge as it had so many times in the past. Another broke down in tears of joy and said he had thought he was alone, but now he knows he has real friends and allies against his spiritual foes. One woman said to me, "I am opposed to war, but I never guessed that I would desire to become a master warrior, to fight the real enemy in perhaps the only noble battle, the battle against my self. And I couldn't have imagined actually winning that battle, but it gets better every day. Here's to victory!"

Use this book to help you face your spiritual enemies. Find allies who will go into battle with you, and explore together how to take control of your lives. Allow for the possibilities your God has in store for you, and give yourself the opportunity to know spiritual integrity, love, and freedom. If you do so, you not only help yourself, but by walking with intention and nobility, as a true spiritual warrior, you make this world a better place for all of us.

Stahyu! Be strong!

CHAPTER 13

Tasks

1. Make a commitment to live, represent, and stand up for what you consider to be the good and authentic Way. What does that look like? What pledge can you make to walk in this Way? Make a pledge.

2. Examine your life. Do you approach the spiritual battle with calm, determination, persistence, humility, and an openness to divine leading? Which qualities do you demonstrate well? Which need work? Take steps to improve in the areas which need work.

3. What is the voice you send as you walk the path of life? What would you like it to communicate? How can you walk your life in a sacred manner? What tracks would you like to leave behind?

Appendix 1

A Guide for Conducting
Spiritual Warfare Fellowship Groups

Opening Remarks: Welcome to our spiritual warfare fellowship. Spiritual warfare is not about fighting against others, or fighting for any particular cause, religious belief, or association. It is a personal spiritual battle against the demons, destructive tendencies, addictions, compulsions, evils, and falsehoods within each individual. It is a very real battle which takes place in the minds, hearts, and lives of all those who choose to live spiritually. This fellowship supports each individual in fighting these battles, in preserving hope, in offering companionship on the spiritual battlefield, and in helping to pave the way toward spiritual victory.

Because of the personal nature of these battles, it is absolutely necessary to keep everything that is said in these sessions in confidence and to reserve judgment against others. No one wins every spiritual battle, but one can find healing, grow in spiritual strength, and achieve lasting victory if given a safe place to share what is going on inside and an opportunity to learn and to grow. It is our hope that this fellowship will be such a safe and sacred place.

In order to create this safe place, abide by these basic guidelines during our sessions:

1. What is said here stays here.

2. You can choose to pass when it is your time to talk.

3. Be considerate of others, in sharing equal time
*   for speaking.*

4. Do not interrupt others who are speaking.

5. Do not offer advice.

6. Do not attempt to "fix" another's "problems" inside or outside of the group.

7. Reserve judgement and become a caring listener.

Through dedication to your own personal spiritual work and the support of this fellowship, may you gain victory over your spiritual enemies within and find wholeness, spirituality, and inner peace.

Sharing the Struggle: Review the tasks which were suggested in the previous session. (Tasks are suggested at the end of each chapter.) Each spiritual warrior shares any insights or discoveries in performing one of the tasks chosen in the previous session.

Reading: A volunteer reads a chapter from *The Art of Spiritual Warfare*, dealing with the particular subject the group is working on that session.

Sharing the Wisdom: Spiritual warriors share any insights from the reading and how it applies to their particular circumstances and life experience.

Choosing a New Task: Review the tasks recommended at the end of the chapter for the week. Each spiritual warrior chooses a task to focus on in the coming week. Remind the group to be ready at the next session to report on their experiences of practicing these tasks.

Closing Huddle and Prayers: Spiritual warriors stand and clasp hands. Individuals may offer a prayer.

Appendix 2

Spiritual Warfare Effectiveness Training
A weekend of adventure, spiritual growth, fellowship, and learning

Accessing the Warrior Within

Spiritual warfare is a reality—there isn't a person on the planet who does not do battle with inner demons. Awakening the warrior within, learning techniques of inner combat, mastering the self, accessing higher powers, and adopting a mission-oriented path of life are the means of gaining inner victory and lasting spiritual peace. This weekend is devoted to the development of the warrior psyche, connecting the warrior both to the spirit and the earth, and to the fellowship of spiritual warriors.

Adventure and Spiritual Discovery

Spiritual Warfare Effectiveness Training is a learning experience and an adventure. The warrior experiences kinship with the earth, learning to reintegrate with nature and to consciously walk, observe, play, and graciously live within it. Participants have an opportunity through many processes, including guided imagery, ritual, and play, to experience the courage, fellowship, honor, and heroic nature of the spiritual warrior. Participants also explore the vast and awesome landscape within as they are given the opportunity to awaken to higher realities of spirit, including a greater awareness of the Creator, which offers a deep sense of meaning to their lives well beyond the weekend itself.

Who Will Benefit?

Anyone will benefit from this training, especially those with an open mind and a quest for spirituality and a connection with the earth and sky. Those who have experienced other weekend adventures and training will especially benefit because they have a firm base upon which to grow spiritually.

For more information:

Write to Spiritual Warfare Effectiveness Training,
P.O. Box 267, Huntingdon Valley, PA 19006, or e-mail
SWETINFO@aol.com.

If you would like to contact Grant Schnarr with questions or are interested in acquiring him for a speaking engagement, write to:

Grant Schnarr
P. O. Box 743
Bryn Athyn, PA 19009
E-mail: GRSchnarr@aol.com
www.spiritual-recovery.com

Notes

CHAPTER 1. SPIRITUAL ASSESSMENTS

1. *Shambhala: The Sacred Path of the Warrior* by Chogyam Trungpa, © 1984. Reprinted by arrangement with Shambhala Publications, Inc. Boston, www.shambhala.com

CHAPTER 2. THE WEAPONS OF SPIRITUAL WARFARE

1. Reprinted from *Being Peace* (1987) by Thich Nhat Hanh with permission of Parallax Press, Berkeley, California.

2. Lorenzo Scupoli, *Unseen Warfare* (New York: St. Vladimir's Seminary Press, 1995), 206.

3. Emanuel Swedenborg, *Arcana Coelestia* (reprint, London: Swedenborg Society, 1993), 541.

4. Excerpted from *Wisdom of the Native Americans*, edited by Kent Nerburn © 1991. Reprinted with permission of New World Library, Novato, CA 94949, www.nwlib.com

CHAPTER 3. COMBAT STRATEGY

1. Carlos Castaneda, *The Wheel of Time: The Shamans of Ancient Mexico, Their Thoughts about Life, Death and the Universe* (Los Angeles: LA Eidelona Press, 1999), 19.

2. Ibid., 267.

CHAPTER 4. STRATEGIC DISPOSITIONS

1. Excerpted from *Tao Te Ching by Lao Tzu, A New English Version* with Foreword and Notes by Stephen Mitchell. Translation copyright © 1988 by Stephen Mitchell. Reprinted by permission of HarperCollins Publishers, Inc.

2. Emanuel Swedenborg, *Doctrine of Life* (reprint, London: Swedenborg Society, 1954), 68.

3. Trungpa, *Shambhala*, 44.

4. Nhat Hanh, *Being Peace*, 35.

5. From *The Zen Way to the Martial Arts* by Taisen Deshimaru, translated by Nancy Amphoux, copyright © 1983 by Taisen Deshimaru. Used by permission of Dutton, a division of Penguin Putnam Inc.

CHAPTER 5. *CREATING SPIRITUAL ADVANTAGE*

1. *Tao Te Ching, A New English Version*, 27.

2. Castaneda, *The Wheel of Time*, 97.

CHAPTER 6. *EMPTINESS AND FULLNESS*

1. Emmanuel Swedenborg, *Divine Providence*, trans. W. F. Wunsch (West Chester, Pa.: Swedenborg Foundation, 1996), 151.

2. *Dhammapada: The Sayings of the Buddha*, trans. Thomas Byrom (Boston: Shambhala Publications, 1993), 7.

CHAPTER 7. *SURVIVING SPIRITUAL STRUGGLE*

1. *The Dhammapada*, trans. F. Max Muller (1870); quoted in *Religions of the World* (New York: St. Martin's Press, 1983), 191.

2. *Dhammapada: The Sayings of the Buddha*, trans. Thomas Byrom, 95.

3. See task number three at the end of chapter one.

4. T'ai Kung, *Six Secret Teachings*, as quoted in *The Art of the Warrior: Leadership and Strategy from the Chinese Military Classics*, trans. and ed. Ralph D. Sawyer (Boston: Shambhala Publications, 1996), 84.

CHAPTER 8. *ADAPTATIONS*

1. Helen Keller, *Light in My Darkness* (West Chester, Pa.: Swedenborg Foundation, 1995), 160.

2. Teedyuscung in *Native American Wisdom*, ed. Kent Nerburn and Louise Mengelkoch, 25–6.

3. Miyamoto Musashi, *A Book of Five Rings: The Classic Guide to Strategy* (Woodstock, N.Y.: Overlook Press, 1982), 54.

CHAPTER 9. *STRATEGIC MANEUVERING*

1. Thomas Carlisle, "Sir Walter Scott," *London and Westminster Review* (no. 12, 1838).

2. Castaneda, *The Wheel of Time*, 144.

CHAPTER 10. *TRAVERSING THE TERRAIN*

1. Emanuel Swedenborg, *Divine Love and Wisdom* (reprint, New York: Swedenborg Foundation, 1976), 26.

2. Reprinted from *Black Elk Speaks*, by John G. Neihardt, by permission of the University of Nebraska Press. Copyright 1932, 1959, 1972, by John G. Neihardt. Copyright © 1961 by the John G. Neihardt Trust.

3. *Tao Te Ching, A New English Version*, 36.

CHAPTER 11. *BATTLEGROUNDS*

1. Sir Walter Scott, *Familiar Quotations*, ed. John Bartlett (Boston: Little Brown & Company, 1938), 311.

CHAPTER 12. *SPIRITUAL FIRE*

1. *Tao Te Ching, A New English Version*, 78.

2. Ibid., 44.

CHAPTER 13. *THE WAY OF THE WARRIOR*

1. Dan Millman, *Way of the Peaceful Warrior: A Book that Changes Lives* (Tiburon, Calif.: H. J. Kramer, Inc., 1991), 37.

2. *Black Elk Speaks*, 4.

3. Nhat Hanh, *Being Peace*, 47.

Bibliography

Bhagavad Gita. Translated by W. J. Johnson. New York: Oxford University Press, 1994.

Castaneda, Carlos. *The Wheel of Time: The Shamans of Ancient Mexico, Their Thoughts about Life, Death and the Universe*. Los Angeles: LA Eidolona Press, 1999.

Dhammapada: The Sayings of the Buddha. Translated by Thomas Byrom. Boston & London: Shambhala Publications, 1993.

DeMallie, Raymond, and Elaine Jahner, eds. *Lakota Belief and Ritual*. Lincoln: University of Nebraska Press, 1991.

Deshimaru, Taisen. *The Zen Way to the Martial Arts*. New York: Penguin Books USA, Inc., 1982.

Fields, Rick, ed. *The Awakened Warrior*. New York: G. P. Putnam's Sons, 1994.

Koran. Translated by N. J. Dawood. New York: Penguin Books USA, Inc., 1956.

Krause, Donald. *The Art of War for Executives*. New York: The Berkley Publishing Group, 1995.

Lao Tzu. *Tao Te Ching*. Translated by Stephen Mitchell. New York: Harper Collins Publishers, Inc., 1988.

———. *The Way of Life According to Lao Tzu*. Translated by Witter Bynner. New York: The Berkley Publishing Group, 1944.

Millman, Dan. *Way of the Peaceful Warrior*. Tiburon, Calif.: H. J. Kramer, Inc., 1991.

Moore, Robert, and Douglas Gillette. *King, Warrior, Magician, Lover: Rediscovering the Archetypes of the Mature Masculine*. San Francisco: Harper Collins, 1990.

———. *The King Within: Accessing the King in the Male Psyche*. New York: Avon Books, 1992.

————. *The Warrior Within: Accessing the Knight in the Male Psyche.* New York: Avon Books, 1993.

Musashi, Miyamoto. *A Book of Five Rings: The Classic Guide to Strategy.* Translated by Victor Harris. Woodstock, N.Y.: Overlook Press, 1982.

Native American Wisdom. Philadelphia: Running Press, 1994.

Nerburn, Kent, and Louise Mengelkoch, eds. *Native American Wisdom.* Novato, Calif.: New World Library, 1991.

Scupoli, Lorenzo. *Unseen Warfare.* Edited by Nicodemus of the Holy Mountain and revised by Theophan the Recluse. Translated by E. Kadloubovsky and G. E. H. Palmer. New York: St. Vladimir's Seminary Press, 1995.

Sun Tzu. *The Art of War.* Translated by Thomas Cleary. Boston: Shambhala Publications, 1991.

————. *The Art of Warfare.* Translated by Roger Ames. New York: Ballantine Books, 1993.

Swedenborg, Emanuel. *Arcana Coelestia.* 12 vols. Translated by John Elliott. London: Swedenborg Society, 1986–1998.

————. *Charity:The Practice of Neighborliness.* 2nd ed. Translated by W. F. Wunsch. Revised and edited by W. R. Woofenden. West Chester, Pa.: Swedenborg Foundation, 1995.

————. *Divine Love and Wisdom.* 2nd ed. Translated by J. C. Ager. West Chester, Pa.: Swedenborg Foundation, 1995.

————. *Divine Providence.* 2nd ed. Translated by W. F. Wunsch. West Chester, Pa.: Swedenborg Foundation, 1996.

————. *Four Doctrines.* 2nd ed. Translated by J. F. Potts. West Chester, Pa.: Swedenborg Foundation, 1997.

Trungpa, Chogyam. *Shambhala: The Sacred Path of the Warrior.* Boston & London: Shambhala Publications, 1984.

QUEST BOOKS

are published by

The Theosophical Society in America,

Wheaton, Illinois 60189-0270,

a branch of a world fellowship,

a membership organization

dedicated to the promotion of the unity

of humanity and the encouragement of the study

of religion, philosophy, and science, to the end that

we may better understand ourselves and our place

in the universe. The Society stands for complete

freedom of individual search and belief.

For further information about its activities,

write, call 1-800-669-1571,

e-mail olcott@theosophia.org,

or consult its Web page:

http://www.theosophical.org

The Theosophical Publishing House
is aided by the generous support of
THE KERN FOUNDATION,
a trust established by Herbert A. Kern
and dedicated to Theosophical education.